SCOTNOTES
Number 22

Matthew Fitt's
But n Ben A-Go-Go

Christine Robinson

Association for Scottish Literary Studies 2008

Published by
Association for Scottish Literary Studies
Department of Scottish Literature
7 University Gardens
University of Glasgow
Glasgow G12 8QH
www.asls.org.uk

ASLS is a registered charity no. SC006535

First published 2008

A CIP catalogue for this title is available from the British
Library

ISBN 978-0-948877-67-4

The Association for Scottish Literary Studies
acknowledges the support of the Scottish Arts Council
towards the publication of this book

Typeset by AFS Image Setters Ltd, Glasgow
Printed by Bell & Bain Ltd, Glasgow

CONTENTS

All page references are to the edition published by Luath Press Ltd.

SCOTNOTES

Study guides to major Scottish writers and literary texts

Produced by the Education Committee
of the Association for Scottish Literary Studies

Series Editors
Lorna Borrowman Smith
Ronald Renton

THE ASSOCIATION FOR SCOTTISH LITERARY STUDIES aims to promote the study, teaching and writing of Scottish literature, and to further the study of the languages of Scotland.

To these ends, the ASLS publishes works of Scottish literature; literary criticism and in-depth reviews of Scottish books in *Scottish Studies Review*; short articles, features and news in *ScotLit*; and scholarly studies of language in *Scottish Language*. It also publishes *New Writing Scotland*, an annual anthology of new poetry, drama and short fiction, in Scots, English and Gaelic. ASLS has also prepared a range of teaching materials covering Scottish language and literature for use in schools.

All the above publications are available as a single "package", in return for an annual subscription. Enquiries should be sent to:

ASLS, Department of Scottish Literature, 7 University Gardens, University of Glasgow, Glasgow G12 8QH. Telephone/fax +44 (0)141 330 5309, e-mail **office@asls.org.uk** or visit our website at **www.asls.org.uk**

EDITORS' FOREWORD

The *Scotnotes* booklets are a series of study guides to major Scottish writers and literary texts that are likely to be elements within literature courses. They are aimed at senior pupils in secondary schools and students in further education colleges and colleges of education. Each booklet in the series is written by a person who is not only an authority on the particular writer or text but also experienced in teaching at the relevant levels in schools or colleges. Furthermore, the editorial board, composed of members of the Education Committee of the Association for Scottish Literary Studies, considers the suitability of each booklet for the students in question.

For many years there has been a shortage of readily accessible critical notes for the general student of Scottish literature. *Scotnotes* has grown as a series to meet this need, and provides students with valuable aids to the understanding and appreciation of the key writers and major texts within the Scottish literary tradition.

Lorna Borrowman Smith
Ronald Renton

INTRODUCTION

But n Ben A-Go-Go is no ordinary novel. On the one hand
it is a violent and sensational thriller, a piece of science
fiction and action-packed escapism; on the other, it is often
almost poetic in its language and structure. It is
meticulously crafted, incorporates broad humour, verbal
wit and social satire and follows characters of epic nobility
and depravity through a nail-biting plot with many twists
and turns. Although it wears its learning lightly, this
book draws on literary and oral story-telling conventions
stretching back to classical times.

Not only that, this novel is groundbreaking in its use of
the Scots language. Students of literature are accustomed
to dealing with English texts and instinctively use their
knowledge of English language to deduce all manner of
things about characters from the way they speak. From
their knowledge of South British Standard English (SBrE),
they can deduce whether a character is speaking formally
or informally. Speech other than SBrE has come to be
associated with lower class characters and informal speech.
This is what readers have come to expect from novelists
since the days of Charles Dickens and Sir Walter Scott.
What we have in *But n Ben A-Go-Go* is a novel in a
language other than English, but it is a language which
English speakers will find intelligible. This is the first
language of most Scots but, because it has not traditionally
been supported by the educational system, its use in formal
situations has been in decline since the early eighteenth
century.

But n Ben A-Go-Go is itself a statement about language.
It raises important questions about attitudes to language. It
demonstrates how a living language can expand and grow
into new uses. It defies all the thought police who want to
make spelling rules for Scots and even makes us question
the need for these rules. For Scots speakers and those who
speak no Scots, this book poses questions about the way we
use language and provides an exciting vehicle for studying
the dialects of Scots today and the possible development of
Scots, albeit in an imaginary world in 2090.

PLOT SUMMARY

To reduce the plot to its bare bones, Scotland in 2090 is
mostly under water and the majority of the population live
on floating cities. The hero is Paolo whose wife, Nadia, has
been infected with the virus, *Sangue de Verde* (Senga). She
lies trapped in a living death and can only be released by a
sample of DNA from the person who infected her. Although
he knows that she has been unfaithful to him, Paolo loves
Nadia and is determined to track down her lover to obtain
the necessary DNA. He is tormented by the strong proba-
bility that this man is his own father, Diamond Broon. His
work apparently sends him in pursuit of a dangerous
employee who is absent from duty. As the book progresses,
the reader and Paolo begin to pick up clues which indicate
that all is not as it seems. First he notices that Lars, the
absentee, is behaving in an unusually determined way and
we discover that he has been paid to give Paolo a message.
This one word message, 'Nadia', is enough to make him
follow Lars, come what may. Lars thus becomes the tool
whereby Paolo is lured into the virtual world of VINE where
his next message can be passed mysteriously to him. It
takes him to see his father's old accomplice, Sark, who
gives him another message, this time sending him in search
of his father who has escaped from prison. After overcoming
such difficulties as swimming a sea in a storm, killing a wild
beast, suffering the dangerous rays of the sun and being
captured by a group of rebel tourists, he is rescued from the
tourists by a police lieutenant, Vermont, who believes she
has been sent to prevent Paolo from killing his father.
Together, they reach his father and Paolo has to go into
VINE in order to bring him back. Too late he discovers that
his father had been manipulating him all along because he
wanted to use Paolo as an organ donor. The policewoman
discovers that the man she knows as her bullying senior
officer is the same man as Sark, Diamond Broon's former
accomplice and rejected lover who seeks revenge against
his former partner. Paolo is rescued in the nick of time and
a sample of DNA from his father allows Nadia to die.

In parallel with the main plot, we follow Diamond

Broon, making his first, virtual escape from prison, in mind only, into VINE to meet Sark, and then physically escaping to his old luxury home, *But n Ben A-Go-Go*.

CHARACTERS

In *But n Ben A-Go-Go*, the plot hangs on a succession of burning, sizzling and festering relationships. The complexity of Paolo's psychological make-up and the depth of Diamond's depravity provide interesting studies of human nature. Sometimes the reader is given insights into the thoughts and feelings of the characters and they can also be judged by their actions. The moral climate of the world they live in affects the characters' behaviour and motivations.

There are various options open to an author as to how character is revealed. The author can let a third person narrator tell us about the character and, since we tend to believe what a narrator says, we usually take that information at its face value. Fitt does not allow the narrator to give lengthy psychoanalytical descriptions of his characters. He takes more subtle approaches.

In this novel, the narrator often lets us see indirectly through the eyes of the character, while still seeming to narrate in the third person. This can often be signalled by moving closer to the way the character would speak and referring to time and space as the character would perceive them. For example, on p37, the narrator is speaking but the vocabulary and syntax are much more in keeping with Broon's voice than that of the narrator. The first indication of this is 'Some kinna malfunction jaloused Broon.' There is no punctuation to indicate that this is direct speech and yet it does not take the form of indirect speech: 'Broon jaloused that there was some kinna malfunction'. The use of the sentence fragment 'Some kinna malfunction' suggests Broon's actual thoughts. The question, 'Wis the Java feart tae?' is Broon's, not the narrator's. Broon is admitting his fear to himself. The vocabulary, 'scagged-oot' and 'keech', for example, is more typical of Broon than of the narrator. What is going on in this passage is a technique that authors quite often use; it is a half-way house between narration and direct speech, allowing the reader to see through a character's eyes and enter the character's thoughts in situations where it would be inappropriate to allow the character to reveal his or her own thoughts in speech.

This brings us to another way to learn about a character, by listening to what a character says about himself or herself. This information has to be evaluated more carefully. Even the way in which individuals think and talk about themselves can make us like them or dislike them. Can we trust someone's self-assessment? How good are we at understanding ourselves? Are we ever guilty of self-deception? Nadia is. Do we ever try to project an image of ourselves to the world that hides what we really feel? Paolo does. Another way to discover what a character is like is to listen to gossip. What do other characters in the book say about him or her? Whether we believe them or not depends on our assessment of those speakers' characters and the nature of their relationships with the character we are studying. Finally, we judge people by their actions. Again, it is possible that someone does the wrong thing for the right reasons, or vice-versa, but, over the course of a novel, a character's actions are a pretty reliable guide to his or her real self.

In *But n Ben A-Go-Go* we are given all these clues to character, presented in different proportions. We see Paolo largely with the help of the narrator and through his own actions. With Nadia, we are allowed intimate eaves-dropping right inside her head. One of the delights of this book is that we are constantly adding to our knowledge of the characters and revising our understanding of them and our opinion of them as details of their lives and motivations unfold, just as we do when we gradually get to know people in real life.

Paolo, the hero, has the qualities that are expected of the hero of an all-action science fiction thriller. He has courage and physical strength together with the mental capacity to push himself to truly heroic achievements.

The very first thing we read about Paolo Stevenson Broon, aged 30, concerns a part of his genetic code and the inherited qualities that come from his straight-laced maternal grandfather. We are told that the Klogs are an east coast family, although the name sounds decidedly Dutch. The Scots word *grippie*, while not too pejorative, definitely suggests meanness. It leads into an increasingly unpleasant portrait of Paolo's grandfather. The description of the family recalls the kind of Scots Presbyterianism we find in Hogg's *Confessions of a Justified Sinner*. These Klogs are members of the *unco guid*, the elect, whose place in heaven is guaranteed. They can look down upon common sinners. Yet theirs is a religion completely devoid of love and compassion. It is a religion of punishment and repression.

We see Paolo at this stage as the product both of his Klog genes and his Klog upbringing, cold-hearted, unable to cry. At the same time, we sense his grief and his helplessness as he empathises with Nadia's agony. Then we begin to suspect a very unKloglike aspect of him as he takes out a little pink rose. We get our first glimpse of his physical size in the contrast between the delicate flower and his large fist and, when he shows the rose 'awkwardly' (p5), we wonder how much of the awkwardness is emotional and how much is physical. We are made aware of the potential conflict between his sentimental passion for Nadia and the Klog repression. There is a redeeming hint here, though, that far from being without feeling, he deliberately uses the Klog crustiness in a positive way to retain his composure in the face of powerful emotions.

Snippets of information are gradually added. Paolo, like the rest of the population, suffers from headaches caused by a virus, which seems to bear a similar relationship to *Sangue de Verde* (Senga) as HIV bears to AIDS. He is a uniformed cyberjanny. Even although we may not be very sure at this point what a cyberjanny's job description may be, we assume it is a fairly lowly post. A few pages later, we get the supplementary information that he is a cyberjanny third class. He certainly does not have money at his disposal, as he cannot afford to pay the expensive lawyer, Aga Dunblane, once Nadia's own money has been used up. In the face of this setback, he resolves to continue by himself, in spite of the awful knowledge that the most likely candidate for the lover that infected his wife is his own father. Nadia's betrayal is no ordinary one and yet, in spite of that, Paolo's love for her remains unshaken. At this point we might be forgiven for thinking of him as a rather ordinary, if very forgiving man, in a very unhappy situation.

Hints about 'Happy Day' from his boss, McCloud, begin to suggest that there has been some kind of criminal activity in Paolo's past and that is the reason for his lowly employment and his lack of favour with the authorities. With his father and Craw, he has caused serious damage to the cyberspace economy. We learn that after his trial he had been ordered to serve in the amphibian fusiliers as an alternative to a hundred months' solitary confinement. His training in this tough regiment has prepared him well for the rigours he undergoes in the course of the novel, in particular, the long and hazardous swim he undertakes. His employment with Clart Central is extremely dangerous and he guesses that, as a result of his implication in the criminal activities on 'Happy Day', a lot of important people would not be sorry to see him dead. This, he surmises, is why he gets sent off after homicidal Danes.

As he sets off in pursuit of Lars, depressed by Nadia's situation and almost overcome with heat, he feels overwhelmed by a spiritual blackness, at the root of which is his loathing for his father. He has neither the time nor the opportunity to give way to this depression because Lars fires a shot through the roof of the funicular cabin that Paolo is travelling in. From this point on, we begin to see Paolo as a man of action, of great physical courage, quick-witted and determined. Part of his heroism consists of facing his innermost fears. He fears disease; he fears the sun and, most of all, he fears what he knows already in his heart, that his father has been his wife's lover.

Physically, he is under constant attack from viral migraines. He is cut off from his supply of pills that keep these headaches under control and this worries him. He fears the long-term effects of not taking these pills. His other constant enemy is the sun. We are reminded of his vulnerability to its rays throughout the novel. In appearance, he is a pale-skinned albino, scarred by operations for skin cancer but still good-looking. He has an apple-shaped birthmark on his forearm, cold blue eyes and bears a facial resemblance to his father.

Mentally, he is able, alert and wary. Craw credits him
with a 'shairp, logical mind' (p111). His first thought when
Lars attacks him is how the Dane knew he was there. He is
aware that he is being manipulated although he does not
guess the real reason. He sees beneath the surface of events
and instantly understands that the destruction of Vermont's
helicopter was no accident.

His physical strength and courage are never in doubt.
All in the course of a day's work, he throws himself out of a
funicular car, 100 metres up, burns himself on the door
handle of the other car, but still hangs on and then slides
down a rope, which is shot through as he descends, and he
crashes though a shed – a very filmic sequence, a James
Bond moment. Then he finds himself looking down the
barrel of a gun and still he is ready for a chase, spurred on
by anger. He sits down with Lars in a busy diner, with more
concern for the other customers' safety than his own,
knowing that a gun is pointed at him under the table. He
pursues his quarry into VINE (taking the appalling risk of
sharing a hypodermic needle to do so) and uses his superior
mental powers to gain an advantage. By this time we are
in no doubt that we are reading about a super-hero, capable
of facing the same kind of super-human challenges as
Odysseus, Jason, James Bond and Batman. He even has a
sense that this is his destiny: 'It suddenly occurred tae
Paolo that he had probably forkent for years aw that wis
aboot tae happen. ... The dream wis nou warslin its wey
towards reality.' (p71).

Like the best of super heroes he has his Achilles' heel.
What kryptonite is to Superman, the sun is to Paolo. He is
emotionally vulnerable as well. This is no suave James
Bond who meets unbelievable dangers and beautiful women
with the same imperturbable smile. Paolo is in love with
Nadia. He empathises deeply with her. He can feel her pain.
When he reaches the point of exhaustion where he almost
stops swimming, 'he could ayewis feel Nadia's pain
stoundin throu his bluid' (p122). His own mind is the source
of horrors that he finds more difficult to face than life-
threatening physical danger. The thought of what might be
underwater in the 'Glen o the Deid' disgusts him and he is

shaken by a childhood memory of bumping into two corpses while swimming the same stretch of water. This bothers him much more than the physical challenge. Even his love for Nadia has to undergo a test. As Paolo considers the significance of the helicopter's destruction, just for a moment, he is physically disturbed by the close proximity of Vermont. When she dresses his wounds, he finds the touch of her hand soothing and is guiltily aware of her body. He pulls away from her.

The degree and nature of his involvement in 'Happy Day' is never made explicit and remains in doubt, even although he was tried and sentenced. He is not a complete innocent. At the tender age of nine he stole exam papers from his headmaster's safe and sold them to senior pupils at his school, but we are not given any reason to suspect that he is a hardened criminal. Quite the opposite. The qualities which are most apparent in him are love, loyalty, courage and even, on occasion, tenderness.

Like the book of which he is the hero, Paolo operates on multiple levels. He is not just a symbol of heroism or a convenient carrier for the plot, although he is both of these things. He is the man of action, the victim of manipulation by his father, the legend, the sufferer of a more than human burden of grief and the survivor against all the odds. He is both a Klog and a Broon but he has a capacity for love, compassion and even romance that does not come from either his Klog genes or from the Klog part of his up-bringing and, as Vermont, who is probably in the best position to judge, finally realises, the only similarity between Paolo and his father is their mental strength and tenacity. His experiences in his youth at But n Ben A-Go-Go seem to have developed self reliance in him and a love of the outdoors. Living there in a decadent atmosphere of sex, drugs and cybercrime, he has remained remarkably uncorrupted, perhaps because of the Calvinistic Klog side of him.

Desmond (Diamond) Broon, father of Paolo, is introduced to us as a master criminal. He is a raider of data vaults and is widely credited with being the inventor of the

narcotic, 'lugdrug', although in fact he stole the patent.
His criminal activities seem to have been widely varied
over the course of forty years. Right away we are warned
that he has an ungovernable megalomania. He is in prison
at Inverdisney Timeshare Penitentiary, where his legendary
wealth still guarantees him power and allows him an extremely comfortable lifestyle in a well-furnished penthouse
cell. Just as Paolo is a larger than life hero, Broon is drawn
as an arch-villain. There is more than a hint of the comic
book 'baddie' in his ability to run, from his jail, a private
army which can threaten his debtors on the outside, and in
his ownership of real estate on Mercury. His ill-gotten gains
are almost beyond imagining. This is no petty criminal.
The long arm of Diamond Broon reaches into the highest
level of governments across the globe. It is not surprising
that he has an almost unshakeable faith in himself.

At the start of the novel, he is one week away from his
70th birthday and has a very short time to live. He reckons
he can overcome age, infirmity and even death.

Diamond Broon is a hard man. He rules his coterie of
hangers-on with a rod of iron and they are obviously afraid
of his power. He is a cynical but shrewd judge of human
nature. The Diamond knows his son well and counts on
Paolo's love for Nadia. He knows that Paolo will believe
Sark and will be prepared to undergo all manner of hard-
ships to reach But n Ben-A-Go-Go. He has no compunction
about putting his son through torment before finally killing
him to save himself.

He is, as he describes himself, 'an awfie, awfie bad man'
(p193). His intention from the start has been to use his son
to renew his own life and strength. He carries out this
macabre and selfish scheme with meticulous, if devious,
planning. The remorse he feels is so small as to be
negligible. He feels a 'footerie particle of guilt', nothing
that a couple of hours of accelerated sleep couldn't disperse
(p52). By quantifying the degree of guilt that Broon feels,
Fitt does not give us any room to wonder whether Broon
has a better self. If there is any decency in the man at all, it
is literally a shred. The narrator describes him as 'sleekit'
(p21), a word that encapsulates Broon's underhand cunning.

Broon's power does not come from wealth alone. He controls people by love as well as fear. He is charismatic. Nadia is besotted by him. Although she is a highly intelligent woman, she is sufficiently dazzled by him to be blind to his ulterior motives. He is her rough diamond. Power is sexy. Nadia's feelings are entirely credible. He does admit to having felt something for her: 'We saw things in each anither' (p189), but, in spite of this, he deliberately infected her in order to have the power to summon Paolo when he needed him and this admission of attraction to Nadia is made to Paolo in a field of miniature roses, signifying the promiscuous nature of his fleeting affections. He gave a bonsai rose to all his 'lowps'. In referring to his sexual partners as 'lowps', he reduces the act to an impersonal coupling without any emotional involvement. He talks of stealing youth for himself as if he is selfishly taking youth away from his young lovers. Nevertheless, the passionate love that he inspires in Sark is so great that, when it is rejected, it turns to a hatred that knows no bounds and drives Sark to seek revenge. His followers are obviously motivated by money, and he has no illusions about that, but there does seem to be a genuine devotion on the part of Mojo. As well as charisma, he has a well-developed sense of humour, even if some of his jokes are thoroughly sick.

Although it is plain from the state of his health and from his inability to cope in Cowp without Java 5 that he is failing, his power is still awesome and he still inspires fear. In his last visit to VINE, he puts Paolo through another set of tests demonstrating that he himself still has the mental powers to keep control in VINE. He subjects Paolo to severe mental torture making him witness his own birth, Nadia seemingly alive and Nadia kisted. He plays mind games with Paolo for control of the virtual environment. Physically, he must once have had a certain attractiveness although he is now decrepit. He remains vain about his appearance. It upsets him greatly that Mojo has to carry him during their escape from Inverdisney and he hopes that no one sees him in such an undignified situation. His vanity is revealed again by the film-star appearance that he elects to have for

his virtual body. His false teeth become an amusing detail
of his concern for his appearance. The fact that he needs
them at all reflects his age and infirmity. He spits his expensive RealTime dentures into a bowl and when he assumes
a virtual body, he still sports 'immaculate wallies' (p181).

Broon's speech is distinctive. It is the abrasive coarse
wit of a hard man. In fact Fitt creates a kind of late twenty-
first century slang for him from the 1960s and 1970s: 'dig'
(p24) and 'zeds' (p101), made up words like 'shoodaboy'
(p195) and compounds such as 'mega-numptie' (p101). He
also speaks 'DJese' (p24), a mixture of Black English and
Scots. He and Java 5 between them are responsible for most
of the highly creative terms of abuse in the novel. He often
speaks of himself in the third person, 'The Diamond peys
guid siller' (p24) or 'Ah am the Diamond Broon' (p181),
another indication of his megalomania.

Right at the start of the novel we are warned of Broon's
megalomania, but even after we have seen him control,
humiliate and torment Paolo, the sheer enormity of his
intention to use Paolo for a Direct Organ Transfer comes as
a shock. But he is so convinced of his own power that he
thinks he controls everything. It is therefore a moment of
great intensity when he suddenly realises that Sark has
been in control all along. The man he thought of as his
junior partner set up 'Happy Day' in order to kill him.
Broon never suspected that he was a policeman. Finally,
Sark, another of his rejected lovers, has power of life and
death over him. It is Broon's monumental pride in his own
power that makes the revelation so cataclysmic. To Sark's
deceptions there is added the irony that the best advice
Broon could give his son was 'Trust naebody ... Dinna trust
a livin sowel' (p191).

The nickname 'Diamond' suits him well. It is just the
kind of nickname a gangster would have. He would like it
because it flatters his vanity; diamonds sparkle, they are
symbolic of wealth and glamour and superiority. They are
also cold and hard.

James Sark is presented to us as Diamond Broon's
accomplice and partner in crime. Broon sees him as his

inferior, the junior partner. He seems to remember having had a sexual liaison with Sark, but it obviously did not matter much to Broon who has had so many sexual partners. Broon thinks of him reductively as 'his wee tag-alang pal' (p54). The narrator tells us he is younger than Broon and they had made a good team. Very significantly, the narrator tells us, 'even in thae early days the Sark could hide onythin fae onybody' (p53).

We are given to understand that Sark has been in hiding all the time that Broon has been in prison. When we first meet him, Paolo perceives him as pale and ill-looking and we, like all the other characters, are completely taken in by Sark until the final chapter.

Sark, like Senga (see below), is described as a mole. A mole is an 'underground agent'. This is why the meta-phorical name 'mole' is often given to that kind of spy who works within the ranks and tries to destroy an organisation from within. The mole, literally and metaphorically, 'under-mines'. When we stop to think about it, we have a whole range of dead metaphors that the image of the mole can bring back to life. The nickname for the initial stage of the virus that causes Senga is the 'mowdie', short for *mowdie-wart*, the Scots word for a mole. Just as the disease burrows its way unseen round the body and through society and just as the virus is always there in the book, a presence unseen but consciously felt, so the presence of Sark lurks below much of the plot of *But n Ben A-Go-Go*. He is like a disease that goes largely undiagnosed until the dénouement. Sark is one of several reasons for reading the book twice. On the second reading, the clues become apparent. There are plenty of warning signs.

Sark remains something of a mystery. He lives a life of such constant deceit that we are never sure when we are seeing the real character. When he meets Broon in The Café o the Twa Suns, he seems pale and gaunt in appearance and is sick of Czech beer. We get the impression that he has been hiding there for a long time, but we are left to imagine the rest of that encounter. (In Bonnie Lemon's he is still frail, arthritic and ill and he claims to have spent ten years on a Russian made life-support in Siberia, so we are left a little confused as to his actual whereabouts.) Although Paolo addresses him as 'uncle' there is obviously no love lost between them. He knows Sark well enough not to trust him and is curious to know why Sark is willing to act as errand boy for Broon since he believes it is Broon's fault that Sark is a wanted man. He seems to have been on the run for fifteen years, although 'Happy Day' was only ten years earlier.

There is a moment, though, when an earlier relationship between Paolo and Sark is glimpsed. He taught Paolo to swim. Sark leaves Paolo with the advice: 'Soom wi yer hert an soom wi yir mind an ye'll aye win the far shore' (p84). If this is a lesson that Paolo learned from Sark as a child, it has stood him in good stead.

There is something odd about the meeting with Sark in Bonnie Lemon's. Paolo does not trust the evidence of his own eyes and there is a kind of 'recognition' scene. (The recognition scene is a common motif, especially in classical literature. Odysseus, for example is recognised by his nurse when he returns after the Trojan war and his long voyage home when she sees a scar on his leg.) In this case, Sark knows about Paolo's birthmark. Nevertheless, Paolo is still as distrustful as Hamlet was of his father's ghost. Indeed there are several references to Sark as a ghost. At his first appearance, he is an 'apparition' (p81). When Paolo talks to Vermont about the meeting, he describes Sark as a cyberbogle (p171).

The next time Sark appears it is as his alter ego, Craw, although the reader is not yet party to this deception. He interrupts Vermont's domestic life to summon her to his office with 'nae breeks or panties' (p96). He uses her as a sexual object but does not touch her. He looks at her and she finds it deeply offensive. When she does not comply, he sends her a sexually explicit video with his head and hers superimposed upon the heads of a copulating couple. She sees his attentions as her road to promotion and tries to put up with his abuse until he asks her to put pink, fluffy handcuffs on. Her refusal brings proof that Craw will not be crossed. He sends his men to beat her up and leave her in the handcuffs.

It is during Vermont's encounter with Craw in his office that we really begin to notice Craw's North-East dialect. For all his apparent power, he seems to be physically afraid of Vermont when she stands up to him and his complexion is described as 'peeliewally'(p109), which, in hindsight, makes it compatible with what we know of Sark's appearance. By the end of the interview, the North-East dialect is well established in the reader's mind as being associated with Craw.

Although Craw and Sark both disappear from the narrative for a bit, he is still in control. Vermont's men are in reality Craw's spies. The first point at which Craw and Sark really come together is in the image that Vermont sees in Nadia's record of visitors. Craw has visited her only an hour after her kisting. He clearly has had access to inside information. His long arm reaches to Gleann na Marbh to destroy the helicopter.

Craw does not seem to be widely known in Ceilidh. Vermont had not heard of him until she was promoted to lieutenant. When she makes enquiries, nobody in Ceilidh has heard of him and his photograph is not in the database, although he occupies an office on the nineteenth floor of Ceilidh Command and wears a Ceilidh uniform. She concludes that he must be one of the Port elite and a very powerful and dangerous man but, for the reader, his exact status always remains in doubt. We can imagine Craw enjoying the irony of Sark, the criminal fugitive, being studied for a whole semester at the police academy.

The reader is left in no doubt of Craw's evil power and it is therefore one of the highlights of the book when, with a dead kelpie in the corner of the room, Mojo shot, Cairns unconscious, Paolo strapped down and bleeding and Vermont just about to reach the Holy Grail of a DNA sample from Broon, suddenly we hear the chilling north-east voice.

Even after Broon has recognised his old partner, the narrator gives the reader a few moments to make the connection between Craw and Sark by retaining the name Craw until Broon himself gives the game away by addressing him as Sark, to the astonishment of Vermont.

When he tells Broon the whole story, Sark *aka* Craw says
that he has been working undercover for Ceilidh since he
was seventeen and that 'Happy Day' was his idea. Do we
believe him? Was he a Ceilidh mole in Broon's criminal
organisation or was he a criminal mole in Ceilidh, out for
what he could get for himself? Craw is as untrustworthy as
Sark. His final act is certainly in breach of Ceilidh rules.
Killing is not allowed. It is given to Sark to make one of
the most telling comments on the society of the day, where
the constitution shields the citizens from harm but makes
no recognition of and allows no redress for emotional
damage.

As the action draws to a close, we see the full venom of
Sark's need for revenge. He has no hesitation in sticking a
knife in Paolo to help him decide whether or not to murder
Diamond. In the end, there is poetic justice meted out to
him. He sought to avenge himself on a bully against whom
he had a sexual grudge. He is arrested by the lieutenant
whom he himself bullied and sexually abused and he is
confined in his own handcuffs, hoist with his own petard.

Nadia may have retreated into the 'dark soonless fecht wi
Sangue de Verde' (p7), but the reader is still privy to what
remains of her thought processes. Printed white on black
('reversed out'), Nadia's sections are visually cut off from
the rest of the text, just as she herself is cut off from the
world. Her chapter headings look a little like the standing
information on a screen. It is as if we are reading her
thought screen. The grammar is unusual in that there are a
lot of sentence fragments. The first words of Nadia are the
first words of the book. Apart from the title, we have as yet
no clues to work from. Her first word, 'Moarnan', could be
a greeting or it could merely be an indication of the time of
day. Her fragmented grammar creates the impression of
private thoughts, not prose that has been constructed for
someone else to read. The reader soon realises that this is a
stream of consciousness, but it is the writer's use of syntax
that creates this effect. The first short paragraphs of the
opening chapter, separated by *oot*, give the impression of
short bursts of mental activity. As more of the nature of

Nadia's condition is revealed, this is seen to be highly realistic. As the chapter proceeds, the *oot* of a radio communication gives way to single words which seem to represent a pause, a hitch in the mental processes, again suggesting fragmentation of thought.

She seems to have lost track of time. We are told that it is 3.07pm (oddly, not a 24 hour clock) but she thinks it is morning. We are given some idea of what she can sense. She is able to hear. From the fact that she feels power surges, we deduce that she must be on some sort of electrical life support system. She fantasises about a man and decides to call him Pavel. The similarity to the name Paolo is no coincidence. It seems that she has respite from the pain of her illness from time to time. She thinks of it almost with affection.

The second time we get a glimpse inside Nadia's head, she is confused but, from her apparently random thoughts, we can glean a few more clues as to what she is like. We already know from Paolo that she was a lawyer. She is thinking about her work and then her mind goes on to dwell on someone called Morton that she thinks has been on a date with her the night before and who is taking her out again. By this time in the story, we already know that Paolo was and is devoted to her. Why is she thinking about another man? We get a jolt when she thinks, 'whiles I really need tae hurt somebody' (p67). If we were beginning to think that Nadia is not a very nice person, this is confirmation. Then, just for a moment, we believe Paolo crosses her mind; 'I could never hurt the ither ane tho' (p67). She goes back to the backstabbing world of business while Senga sends stabs of pain through her rib cage and legs. The pain takes over and then we are set another puzzle to solve. Why should she say, 'I liked it then ... I yaised tae love ma kenspeckle alien' (p69)? Is it because the disease is her last link with Broon? Is it because, like the pregnancy that she will never experience, it is the secret within her body? Is it because the pain is a form of atonement for her infidelity? We are not told. This chapter is entitled '17' because the virus reaches the peak of its feeding cycle every 17 hours or, at least, in her confused

state with little sense of time, that is when she thinks it
feeds.

Our next meeting with Nadia is given the title 'Lichty
Nichts'. She is addressing Diamond Broon, reminiscing
about skiing holidays in VINE. She thinks there is
something special between them but she is obviously feeling
guilty for deceiving Paolo. She is also worrying about being
found out. She remembers being kisted and, in spite of the
fact that Paolo and she have never had 'old-fashioned' sex,
it is Paolo that she blames for her condition. She had been
led to believe that Diamond was taking weekly tests. From
what we know of Diamond Broon, this tells us that, for a
high-powered lawyer, she is extremely gullible. She accuses
Paolo of unfaithfulness and deceit, which does not accord
at all with what we know of Paolo, having seen what he is
prepared to go through on her behalf. She even briefly
entertains the idea that Paolo might have found out about
her and Diamond Broon and infected her deliberately, but
she dismisses the thought. Then we discover the reason for
this chapter's title. She thinks of late summer evenings with
Paolo in the real world of Lithgow Promenade. She has a
kind of insight into his goodness: 'There wisna a lee in his
face. There was never a moment's soorness on that face'
(p116). Just as we think she is about to see sense, she
decides that Paolo is not man enough to release her and
she puts her faith in Diamond. Her capacity for self-
deception is extreme.

The last time we enter into Nadia's thoughts, in the
chapter entitled 'Tokyo Rose', realisation of the truth has
dawned on her. It is Paolo's face that she has seen at her
screen, not Diamond's. She is still unsure of her feelings for
Paolo and questions whether she married him for himself
or in order to be close to his father. She recognises Diamond
Broon's words for what they were, just 'fancy blethers'
(p141). She recognises Paolo's steadfastness and her own
cowardice in being unable to name her 'Jock Doe'. She tries
to explain why she projected the image of the Bonsai Rose
and, as so often happens in life, his knowledge of the
symbol and hers originated from two separate standpoints.
She saw it as the identifying symbol of the man who gave it

to her. He saw it only as the evocation of betrayal, the Tokyo Rose. Not until he knew that this was his father's habitual gift to his lovers did he understand that it was a clue. At the end, she meant well, but she did not have and had never had the same terms of reference as Paolo.

We get one last painful glimpse of a virtual Nadia on a past skiing holiday with Diamond Broon. Paolo is forced to watch her and listen to her as her words confirm her infidelities.

Vermont is a tall, slim, blonde, ambitious police lieutenant. She lives with her partner Lou and his child Ashka. Ashka's mother appears to have no real interest in her and Vermont feels very maternal towards the little girl, but her feelings towards Lou are less settled. He is jealous and sulky. Her colleagues at work, Watt and Paterson, are sexist bullies who resent her being a better police officer than they are. She is forced by the slightly mysterious Craw to pose for him in various garments while he looks at her for sexual gratification. This disgusts her but he maintains his hold over her with a fake video of her having sex with him, and when she disobeys him, he has her beaten up. She tolerates his behaviour in the hope of promotion. She perceives Craw as being a very powerful member of the Ceilidh executive.

She undertakes a dangerous and responsible mission with few qualms and shows great physical courage and initiative. She is highly intelligent and has a PhD in criminal psychology of which Diamond Broon was the subject.

She is represented as being both strong and vulnerable. Her colleagues upset her, but that is a situation she can deal with. Craw dominates her and, although she tries to fight back, she knows that he has the upper hand psychologically. She is doing a job on an equal basis with men. In her private life, she feels able to make her own decisions. She is physically strong and expected to take on any situation that a man would. Yet the language that Craw uses to her is chosen to put her in an old fashioned, subordinate position. He is making an antifeminist

statement and reducing her to a plaything by calling her
'a bad wee girl' and a 'naughty lassie' (p109). Paolo, too,
from his thirty years of age sees her as 'a slip o a loun's
lass' (p152). Although she has done a deal with the rebel
tourists, she does not have the experience to maintain
control and Paolo has to rescue her. Even when she has a
gun trained on them, she is nervous and does not hold
the gun properly. She is queasy at the sight of Paolo's
gunshot wound, but she deals with it efficiently. Paolo
quickly works out that she is a formidable adversary. He
knows she is cleverer than him, but he has far more
experience. He sets out to shake her self-confidence by
pointing out the downside of the deal she has made with
the tourists. She allows herself to be irritated into the
indiscreet and embarrassing admission that she was thrown
out of her own helicopter.

Vermont grows in the course of the novel. At the start
she is a well-trained police lieutenant. Her instinct is to
obey orders, even when they are unpleasant. There is a
rebellious streak in her but, although she is feisty, she is
untested and is not yet aware of her own limitations. As
she faces extreme situations she experiences fear and self-
doubt and learns how to live with them. Her faith in the
system she works to uphold is shaken. Paolo tells her she is
a creature of procedure and she certainly seems to think
that, if she does things by the book, all the disorder around
her will right itself. Neverthless, when she has to make
decisions in the heat of the moment, she gets Broon's DNA
for Paolo, takes time to reassure him that she has it and,
in spite of being badly shaken by Broon's death, reacts
instantly to the opportunity that Paolo's scream gives her
to overpower Craw. With an exquisite sense of justice and
humour, she restrains him with his own pink handcuffs.

There are the stirrings of tenderness between Paolo and
Vermont. They are conscious of each other's sexuality but,
if Paolo is remarkable for the depth of his love for Nadia
and his fidelity to her, Vermont is remarkable for
understanding and respecting the power of his love. She
knows that his love for Nadia will keep his mangled body
alive until he gets his father's DNA to her. We hope that it

is Vermont standing beside Paolo as Nadia is consigned to
the crematorium.

Senga. Why include a disease among the characters? The
virus is thought of and spoken of by the characters as if it
were animate. Consistently referred to as 'she', the disease
is given a girl's name. Considering the many inversions in
this novel, it may be significant that this destroyer's name
spelled backwards is Agnes, which in Latin means lamb, a
Christian symbol for the Saviour. Nadia thinks of the
renewal of suffering as Senga wakening when she is hungry
and calls her a 'puir wee tyke' (p3). The idea of Senga as
experiencing hunger returns with the narrator's comment
that 'yin micro-guff o Senga would ignite a Green Bluid
pandemic that wid chow its wey throu Port in less than
hauf a day' (p9).

Senga is so infectious that its victims cannot be buried
or cremated. It feeds on the living but escapes from the
body after death to seek a new victim. This is why the
victims are kept alive at Rigo Imbeki; their still-living
bodies keep Senga trapped inside them.

The disease does not start as full-blown Senga. An HIV-
like virus infects the entire population. One symptom of
this is headaches. The MDZ pills, megadiazine 7, distributed
to cyberjannies by the quartermaster at Clart Central, keep
the virus under control. Paolo is unsure how long it is
possible to go without the pills before the body is overcome
by disease. In one case he knows of, a man became in-
curably ill after two weeks without pills. Not all the
population have easy access to MDZ 7; people remortgage
their houses, get into debt, steal and resort to violence in
order to get their hands on the life-prolonging pills. For
such a pandemic disease, public information seems limited.

Although, without drugs, it seems the eventual onset of
the active stage of Senga is inevitable, it is brought about
more rapidly by direct contact with the active stage or by
sexual contact. Sensibly, few people have 'old-fashioned' sex
and virtual sex has become the norm. Women are more
susceptible to infection and there appear to be some people,
like Diamond Broon who are carriers, able to have many

sexual partners without succumbing to the disease
themselves. It does appear, however, that once a person has
become infected and been kisted to contain the infection,
the Senga virus can be neutralised if a sample of the DNA
of the patient's carrier partner can be obtained.

Senga is frequently described in the book using animal
imagery, as a beast hungering, chewing, crawling, creeping.
Like the mole, it burrows unseen as it works its way around
the body The *mowdie* as a reference to the all-pervading
disease burrows its way through the book, and there is one
other 'mole' in the book – Sark.

Minor characters

Aga Dunbar is a very expensive but clever lawyer who
makes a particular effort in Senga cases because her own
husband had been kisted for 15 years. She is an elegant
melano with two Dryland dachas and a passion for smart
clothes. Although she has a reputation for being ruthless,
we see that, in her dealings with Paolo, under her business-
like exterior, she is a compassionate and understanding
woman. She demonstrates this after she has delivered the
bad news to Paolo that her firm can no longer pursue
Nadia's case when her voice softens and she offers Paolo a
drink. When Paolo doesn't meet her eyes, she seems to
know exactly how he is feeling and exits tactfully.

McCloud is Paolo's boss at Clart Central. Pale, spotty,
foul-mouthed and untidy, he seems to spend a lot of time
eating fast food and littering his desk with the remains of
his meals. He sends Paolo off after Lars and we can deduce
from that that he is in the pay of Diamond Broon. He also
arranged for the destruction of Bonnie Lemon's. He could
have been acting on Broon's orders, but the timing, just
before the police, sent by Vermont, got there, suggests that
Craw ultimately controls him as well.

Lars Fergusson is a psychotic Dane who works for Clart
Central and makes something of a habit of not turning up
for work. On this occasion, he is not behaving as he

normally does when he has to be persuaded back to work. Usually he puts up only token resistance. This time, he is harder to catch. He is large, violent, clad in black combat dress with a red Fusiliers beret, and carries a sawn-off magnum. He speaks Scots with a strong Scandinavian accent. Although Danes, like everyone else, do not kill people, Lars seems to revel in violence. At the beginning of one of the Old Norse sagas, the subject of the saga, Egil, is described as a 'berserker'. Lars has a lot of this Viking trait in him.

Cutty Boab is the housebreaker who delivers the experience needle to Diamond Broon. He can be trusted to keep his mouth shut and this is why Broon employs him. He is also expected, for additional payment, to attack Sawney Ip, if Ip shows any sign of bungling.

Sawney Ip is a sharp-nosed, yellow-eyed albino whom Diamond does not trust. He covets Broon's experience needle. Shot by a guard during the escape from prison, he is drowned by Mojo on Broon's instructions because he is unable to travel.

Dr Hans Cairns is the Diamond's clever but unscrupulous medical man and fellow prisoner. He is necessary for Broon's plans but he is not trusted. His bedside manner is not sympathetic. Some of his equipment is a bit old-fashioned; he is still using a mercury thermometer, for example, but he has enjoyed laboratory facilities in the penitentiary, paid for by Broon. His original offence was smuggling discount organ farm hearts from South Africa into Port.

Mojo is the fearless Inuit bodyguard who speaks in broken Scots. He is a big albino man wearing sealskin. Broon trusts him to keep an eye on Cairns and Ip while he is in VINE. Even when Broon is in no state to give commands, Mojo protects Hans Cairns from the kelpie.

Java 5 is another unlikely character since it is a microchip, but it is a microchip which has a personality, speaks in Dundee dialect and has a chapter named after it. A malfunction is given the ambiguously human description of 'a brekdoon' (p37). Diamond Broon for a moment even imagines that it is experiencing fear. Its old age and eventual scrapping are jocularly linked to a kind of microchip afterlife and the whole conceit is brought to an absurd climax with the notion of Java 5 having 'a mystical oot-o-program experience' (p37). Broon regards the chip as an old crony. It is a master of the Scots art of flyting and attacks Broon with poetic streams of abuse. (Flyting is a Scots word meaning scolding or arguing. It was raised to an art form by medieval Scots poets who insulted each other in very sophisticated, but scandalous verse as a court entertainment. The best known of these is the Flyting between Dunbar and his fellow poet, Kennedy, which can be found in any collection of the works of William Dunbar.) Java 5 also seems to have a wicked sense of humour. Some of these characteristics of Java 5 provide comment on our current love-hate relationship with technology. Even the most rational of us have moments when we think that a machine is deliberately annoying us. We want to believe in Java 5 as the embodiment of technological spite.

Paradoxically, the name itself, Java 5, is quite impersonal. It suggests that there were four earlier, and possibly inferior, versions. We are made aware that Java 5 is ready to be scrapped, and no doubt, somewhere, version six or seven exists. Yet we, and Broon, treat it as an animate individual. This is entirely because of its advanced speech technology. The ability of machines to simulate speech has improved enormously in recent years. In most cases, machines, such as in-car satellite navigation systems, are given female voices with non-regional accents, as these are perceived as non-threatening. A male voice with the accent of an industrial city is a casting director's most likely choice to play an aggressive character. Obviously, not all inner-city males are aggressive, but this is a linguistic stereotype that we have come to recognise and accept.

The generation of apparently interactive speech, such as

Java 5 seems capable of, is still very much in its infancy. Yet the possibilities that are even now beginning to open up allow us to believe that a Java 5 could exist in the not too distant future.

Narrator. The narrator is not a character taking part in the action of the novel. Nevertheless, the storyteller is usually a fictional creation and cannot be automatically assumed to hold the same views and opinions as the author. Narrators are often assumed to be omniscient, but, in order to avoid giving away surprise endings, they sometimes have to enter into a kind of conspiracy of ignorance. The narrator of *But n Ben A-Go-Go* keeps the story moving forward at a fast pace. Scenes are vividly pictured but there is never a sense of descriptive passages holding back the story. Although the narrator reveals the inner feelings of characters, no judgements are made. That is left to the reader. This narrator is chameleon-like, unobtrusive, fading into the background and often effectively narrating from the viewpoint of the characters in the action.

GENRE

But n Ben A-Go-Go belongs firmly in the science fiction
genre. As a genre, science fiction gives the reader certain
expectations.

- The science fiction novel is likely to take the form of a
  quest.
- The landscape is likely to be unfamiliar either because
  the novel is set on a different planet or because it is set
  on Earth at a different period from the present, usually at
  some point in the future.
- The practicalities of life are usually mentioned such as
  food, housing and transport.
- A futuristic scenario is generally given credibility by
  extrapolating current trends so that scientific develop-
  ments, for example, can be seen to be advanced models of
  today's technologies.
- There is very often a strong element of social comment,
  usually directed at the society of here and now. A future
  or interplanetary vision of a Utopia may be presented in
  which society has become wise and well-ordered, but a
  Dystopia growing out of the disordered society of today is
  a much more common scenario.

The quest

The quest is a plot line that goes back to the most ancient
story-telling; long before such quests as *Lord of the Rings*,
Raiders of the Lost Ark and *Monty Python and the Holy
Grail*, there were the great quest Romances of the Middle
Ages, such as *Gawain and the Green Knight*, and, before
that, Aeneas went off in search of a place to found Rome,
and Jason went in search of the Golden Fleece. The quest is
the stuff of myth and legend but it has lost none of its
effectiveness as a vehicle for a plot.

The quest, be it for a Golden Fleece or, as in *But n Ben
A-Go-Go*, a sample of DNA is, whether the hero knows it or
not, also a quest for self-knowledge.

The quest generally incorporates a number of traditional
elements: a summons, a journey, sometimes with false or

delayed starts, setbacks and life-threatening struggles along the way, tests of worthiness often culminating in a climactic confrontation with evil forces before the object of the quest is achieved. The object of the quest may be a tangible reward such as an item of great value, it may be a less tangible treasure such as knowledge or spiritual enrichment or it may be a task that must be performed. After a successful outcome, there may be an account of the journey home and, typically, there is the satisfaction of eventual triumph of good over evil and happiness, if not ever after, at least until the sequel!

Many of these elements are present in *But n Ben A-Go-Go*. Paolo's quest is for a sample of DNA to release his lover Nadia from her living death as a victim of the disease known as Senga. The source of the summons is Paolo's father, Diamond Broon, through the intermediaries of Lars and Sark. His tussle with Lars and his meeting with Sark delay the start of his real journey, but once that gets under way, we discover that he is as powerful a swimmer as Beowulf and the kelpie he kills is as fearsome as any Minotaur or Hydra. With the help of a woman (another common factor in quests), he overcomes the embodiment of evil to attain his goal. We do not see the journey home and the ending is not jubilant, but there is no doubt that Paolo's quest is on a heroic scale.

Of time and place
The novel takes place here on Earth, but at a future date and in a much changed landscape. As is often the case with science fiction, an extrapolation of problems already perceived has brought about a cataclysmic event. In the *Planet of the Apes*, written by Pierre Boulle in 1968, space travellers arrive on a war-ravaged planet, only to discover at the very end that they are back on Earth. At the time when *Planet of the Apes* was written, the threat of nuclear war was very real and frightening. Now, at the start of the twenty-first century, the build up of greenhouse gases, the destruction of the ozone layer and threat of global warming hang over the world, as we know it. Daily, we hear evidence of climate change. Fitt sets his novel in the world that these

warnings forecast. We are often reminded that large
icebergs are breaking off the Ross Ice Shelf. We know that
sea levels are rising. Some even now predict disaster.
Before we even open this book, our minds are fully prepared to believe in 'God's Flood'.

It is a fact that the ozone layer has been damaged and
we are bombarded by warnings to protect ourselves from
skin cancer by covering ourselves up and using high factor
sunscreen on exposed areas of our bodies. There are
constant reminders throughout the novel of the devastating
effects of UV rays on pale, unprotected skin. Paolo slaps
on 'Factor Extreme' (p137). A single moment's exposure is
enough to make his feet nip when he takes off his boots and
socks (p143). The mode of torture used by the rebel tourists
is to take off his clothes (p151). This is all chillingly
plausible. The climate is tropical. Even in January the
population of Scotland swelters under a fierce sun and
suffers hurricanes and tropical mists. The UV rays of the
sun are much more dangerous than they are today to pale
skinned *albinos* but the darker skinned *melanos* seem to
have a greater tolerance of the sun.

The Scotland we find in 2090 is very different from that
of today, but we have no problem in understanding the
disaster scenario Fitt presents. The splitting of the Ross Ice
Shelf by volcanic activity in Antarctica has hastened the
thawing of the ice at the South Pole with sudden
catastrophic effects in the year 2039. As explained in the
introductory 'Road Map' (pxiii) the resultant great flood
has covered most of Scotland and inundated a large area of
the world. Only mountainous regions have survived above
water. The cities of Scotland now take the form of man-
made islands, attached to the sea bed. It takes some stretch
of the imagination to picture the futuristic community of
Port, in the twenty-seven floating cities all improbably
anchored to the seabed at the drowned port of Greenock.
The cityscapes that Fitt draws are vivid and dramatic.
Glasgow parish has 'cloodkittlers'. We are asked to imagine
huge high-rise buildings such as the two-thousand-storey
Rigo Imbeki medical centre, with its mile-long corridors,
where Nadia lies a quarter of a mile up, in gallery 1083, and

its external lifts, which are also lounge bars. Technology is advanced. For many inhabitants of Port, life is air-conditioned and comfortable; others, the poor, the immigrant population, live in ugly slums or are homeless.

The surviving parts of the Highlands, renamed the 'Drylands', have become the playground preserve of the very rich, although they are also patrolled by dangerous wild beasts and equally wild and dangerous bands of rebel tourists.

Some domestic details

Some of the domestic technology is already familiar. Broon closes the blinds over his prison window using a remote control as he reclines in his black leather orthopaedic chair. He has a bamboo coffee table. This is cosily familiar.

The eponymous But n Ben A-Go-Go itself, is a far cry from the simple two roomed dwelling that its name suggests. It is a chalet style, three-storey house, built from Canadian pine and Russian steel, with a lot of glass and solar panels, surrounded by outbuildings and helipads. It is heavily defended by automatic snipers. It once had a private zoo but this is now deserted. Inside, it has a dance studio, library, cinema and retro Bavarian bier keller. Luxury is further suggested by the onyx tables and the marble tile flooring. The picture of elegant futurity is counterpointed by the presence of discarded beer cans.

This untidy, expensive comfort contrasts with the hovels in Favela Copenhagen, running on out-of-date technology but kept scrupulously clean.

The food and drink of the future is very international, again extending a trend that is already in evidence. The introduction of something so mundane in a highly imaginative novel is yet another device to create a sense of reality. This is apparent in the mixture of the unfamiliar and the everyday in the comestibles of the future. In 2090 they still drink beer out of cans and whisky (p9), vodka (p16), tequila (p9) and cappuccino (p12) are still available. Daiquiri and Pernod are still around but have bizarrely changed colour, giving us again that sense of simultaneous continuity and change. Rooburgers (p12) are already creeping onto menus

today. The only thing that is new about a soya piece (p38)
or a jeelie baguette (p57) is the naturalisation of their
names. Scots children have been eating jeelie pieces since
time out of mind. Lasagne bridies (p77) provide another
example of the capacity of Scots cookery to embrace foreign
elements just as easily as the vocabulary adopts loan words.
The action of McCloud chucking a yak wishbone (p13)
across his desk is a bit more surprising. In order to have a
wishbone, the yak must have been genetically modified out
of all recognition.

Clothes are not so very different. The kilt is still
worn although Paolo combines it with the practical
keffiyah. Workmen wear overalls. Broon wears an old
T-shirt. Aga Dunblane power-dresses in a suit and high-
heeled shoes.

The world is different, but the day-to-day requirements
for living are unchanged.

Technology

Technological advance is one of the essential elements of
the science fiction genre. Whether it is the spaceship or
the time-machine, some futuristic device transports the
characters to fantastic worlds. The wonder of engineering
that is necessary for the plot of *But n Ben A-Go-Go* is the
communication network VINE. Part of the reader's mind
accepts this as a natural extension of computer games and
the worldwide web in a way that would have been impossible for a reader even 30 years ago. Virtual reality is
already with us. Fitt gives us details that remind us that
this is an integrated network for communication, not just a
device for virtual travel. Messages, in the form of communication midges, fly past the traveller. E-mail has of
course been replaced by v-mail. All kinds of communication
devices have been miniaturised. Laptop computers have
shrunk to palmtops. Vermont, unsurprisingly, wears a
Ceilidh-issue VINE communication bracelet which allows
Ceilidh to track her whereabouts, a sort of combination
between a tagging device and a mobile camera phone. The
silicon tattoo that Paolo had put on his right forearm as a
baby and which communicates through audio, text and hi-

resolution visual, takes us across the threshold from science fact to science fiction.

The other aspect of VINE that demands an imaginative leap on the part of the reader is the sophisticated virtual reality. Entry into VINE is effected by an injection of experience fluid. While the real body lies inert, a microchip navigates the mind through cyberspace and a virtual body is created. The actual appearance of this body seems to be controlled by its user. Broon's virtual body is an improvement on his own. What does not bear too close examination is the degree to which the virtual body can be damaged by other virtual objects. When Broon approaches the Empire State Building at speed, Java 5 suggests that he might be disembowelled. It is certainly possible for injury sustained in VINE to transfer to the RealTime body; Java 5 warns Broon against looking too long at powerful UV lights in case he damages his RealTime retina (p37). Virtual bodies interact with each other but the real skill in this complicated computer game lies in mental agility. It is the power of the mind that controls events in this mental world.

We are not expected to believe that this technology developed overnight. We are told that programs have become obsolete along the way. No one goes on holiday to the old virtual resorts any more and the outmoded but still functional programs have been consigned to a dumping ground in cyberspace. This virtual theme park forms the setting for Broon's and Paolo's meetings with Sark in the Café o the Twa Suns. It is described in some detail in chapter six.

There are degrees or depths of VINE. Access to deep VINE seems to be restricted. Bonnie Lemon's is a halfway house between RealTime and virtual reality. It is not entirely clear where the boundary between RealTime and VINE lies.

Just as there are cracks and joins in the programs that produce virtual reality and as the pixels are visible in the course of illusion being created, the reader moves between total acceptance of the illusion and curiosity about the mechanism behind it. Fitt gives us just enough explanation to suggest a very complex electronic system in a constant

state of obsolescence and development. He engages our belief
sufficiently to make us accept the apparent materialisation
of a letterbox with a note issuing from it as a key device in
the driving forward of the plot.

The blending of real and imaginary to make a convincing
tale has always been a part of the storyteller's art. The
relationship between virtual reality and RealTime in this
book is almost an allegory for the process of creating a
believable fiction. The readers of fiction allow themselves to
be transported into virtual worlds with which they interact
in their imagination. Sometimes, this demands from the
start what the critic and poet Samuel Taylor Coleridge
called 'the willing suspension of disbelief' when the reader
is at once introduced into what is clearly a fantasy world.
Fitt does not ask initially for a suspension of disbelief but
gives us every possible reason to believe that the world he
creates is not just plausible and rational but perhaps even
inevitable. As he sucks us into the world of the novel, he
can then easily persuade us to make the transition to
the much more imaginative and unlikely VINE, where the
characters themselves leave their physical bodies behind
and exist in a world of the mind and imagination, much as
the totally absorbed reader is unaware of immediate
surroundings.

Other advances in engineering have enabled the building
of Port, with its air-conditioned streets and its high-rise
buildings. Nuclear power is available for the rich, oil power
for the poor. Transport, like everything else is a mixture of
known and new technologies. Funicular railways and
helicopters are joined by amphibian trains.

On the medical front, old fashioned mercury thermometers
and hypodermic syringes lag behind gruesome advances in
organ replacement.

Society today and in 2090
Writers such as H. G. Wells and George Orwell have used
their visions of the future to comment on the society of
their time. Matthew Fitt is following in their footsteps.

We can see the roots of 2090's society in our own social
mores. In a world where businesses are becoming in-

creasingly impersonal and where, even in the caring
professions such as nursing, the ability to deal with
technology is seen as more important than the ability to
deal with patients, where globalisation takes power away
from individuals and even from governments, where a
material culture and a sense of self-preservation have all
but eroded altruism and community spirit, many scenes in
this book have strong resonances for the present-day
reader.

One such scene is the account of the press coverage of
the aftermath of Hurricane Elvis in chapter 11. We are left
in no doubt of the extent of the devastation. In each of 27
shelters, a million people, hot, headachy and smelly, watch
TV screens with pictures of fires raging above, of people
struggling in the sea after the collapse of bridges, of the
destruction of essential services, of refugees. These are
images that the reader too has seen on TV. Once the
seriousness of the situation has been established, Fitt then
introduces a glimmer of satirical humour. His TV com-
mentators are 'professional bletherers' and the channel they
blether on is 'Havers Inc.'. The pejorative connotations of
'bletherers' and 'havers' surely make us question the
reliability of the popular media. He returns to the language
of the media with 'aerial and satellite photostills' and
reminds us of the grim picture outside, but what is terri-
fying in close-up, from a distance becomes almost trivial:
from a mile up, the Parishes look like dirty oil drums and,
from space, Port looks like a black eye.

He changes channel for us. The TV channel is now more
of a magazine programme featuring celebrities and, with
the change in channel, Fitt also changes his tone and turns
up the comedy level. He plays with names and incongruity.
First, the great virtual explorer is given a name that is
redolent of macho strength and courage. 'Kirk' makes us
think of the captain of the Starship *Enterprise*; it may even
recall the physically well-developed star of many adventure
films, Kirk Douglas. Che Kirk Wong, however, has
expensive false teeth and a puny physique.

We note with interest that the languages of the broad-
casts are Flemish, American, Arabic and Scots. This has an

interesting parallel in that the royal proclamations in
Scotland were once in Flemish, French, Scots and Latin.
We see that, while Flemish and Scots remain, the great
world languages are American and Arabic. It seems that
American is no longer even a variety of English, but a
language in its own right.

It seems that the Stewart line has been restored to the
throne and royalty continues to fulfil a humanitarian role
in times of national emergency.

The humour reaches a peak with the image of a visiting
football team, come to play Portic Thistle FC in the World
League (an unlikely scenario in itself), seeing out the storm
in a luxury jacuzzi with a ladies' hurling team. The reader
who can suspend disbelief to entertain this mind-boggling
image will have no trouble with the science fiction
inventions of virtual journeying in cyberspace.

Accustomed as we are to the introduction of humour at
times of dramatic climax, we enjoy the jokes and recall how
Shakespeare used humour at the darkest moments of his
tragedies to stop our emotions becoming dulled by excess or
how Londoners used humour during the Blitz in World
War II. But then we read on and find even more horror. Fitt
uses a favourite televisual technique, picturing a disaster
on a large scale by picking out smaller, more manageable
incidents, including the obligatory poignant detail of a
child's toy. Then the whole of Selkirk parish tips over and
is sucked under by the sea. It is impossible to read this
without thinking of the last moments of the Titanic.
Suddenly, we see what this chapter has been about. We are
so accustomed to witnessing human tragedy on TV and film
that we cease to distinguish it from entertainment and can
laugh and joke through the worst news broadcast, distancing
ourselves from the human suffering on the screen. The
inhabitants of Port are desensitised and, to some extent
brutalised, by the life they live, but this is also a comment
on society today. This recognition of ourselves as we are
today, makes Fitt's portrayal of tomorrow's society a totally
reasonable progression.

Chapter 11 occupies a central point in the novel and it
is the only chapter that does not move the plot forward.

This is significant. Although it describes a hurricane, it is itself like a still centre, the eye of the storm in a tempestuous and turbulent story. As such it repays particular study.

It is not the only part of the book where social comment is found. Another similarity between the world of 2090 and the world of today is the social inequality that exists in the Favelas. In the Favela Copenhagen, we see the conditions in which Danish and Norwegian refugees have to live. The Danes keep their Favela very clean, but they use older technology, running their homemade air-conditioners on stolen oil. Their children are hungry. They are not as well provided with cancer clinics as the rest of Port. Their streets are not cooled as they are elsewhere. Schools, hospitals and housing are all far below the accepted standard of the day. As refugees, the Danes have not been made to feel welcome. Other underprivileged immigrant communities are the Flemish on Stranraer Parish and the Moravians on Dumbarton Parish. The Moravians are unhoused.

Even within prisons there is one system for the rich and one for the poor. A rich prisoner is sent as a 'guest' to Inverdisney and can even take the occasional fortnight in another timeshare penitentiary such as Disney Alp. There are less comfortable timeshare penitentiaries such a Kilimanjaro or Popocatapetl, for rich prisoners who do not behave, but the poor prisoner is incarcerated in a bubble below the sea at Submarnock.

The laws of this society are based on laws that have already been enacted or are being debated today. Killing is almost unthinkable except in the most extreme circumstances and corporal punishment is outlawed. In Craw's words, 'Winna punish. Dinna chastise. Ye canna even skelp yer bairns. The Constitution bields us aa fae herm' (p200). When the world has been suddenly depopulated, human life becomes valuable in a political and economic sense. It is a commodity in a way that it has ceased to be on our present overpopulated planet. Perhaps it is this view of human life that makes the civilisation of 2090 strangely lacking in compassion. This is what we see in chapter 11. The law is

enforced by a police force, Ceilidh, whose surveillance
systems are all-pervading and reminiscent of Orwell's
Nineteen Eighty-Four. There are many indications that this
is a disordered society with perverted values. The genetic
manipulation of the kelpie is one such case. The administra-
tion of the day parallels the paternalistic, control-driven,
unloving religion of grandfather Klog.

The suppression of compassion is summed up in the final
chapter when Papa, an attendant in the Rigo Imbeki
Medical Centre, tips Nadia into the crematorium furnace
singing a samba tune and hurrying to get to his friend's
retirement ceilidh. The narrator tells us that 'like the rest
of his generation, he had langsyne cowped aw the brigs tae
his hert' (p206).

Tragi-comedy?

There are laughter and tears in this novel. On the dark
side, Nadia has brought disaster on herself through her
infidelity. The situation in which Paolo finds himself,
through no fault of his own, is truly horrific. The society of
2090 is bleak. There is a strong sense of tragedy running
through the novel and it inspires pity and fear, the two
emotions which are associated with tragedy in its classical
sense. The extent to which the epilogue can be interpreted
as a comforting vision of hope is debateable. Nadia is
allowed to die. That is the whole purpose of Paolo's quest.
It can hardly be seen as an ending that is a positive
affirmation of life. Yet, it is morally right in the sense that
the unnatural prolongation of Nadia's life simply as a way
of keeping the Senga virus under control is a distortion of
any doctrine of the sanctity of human life. The right to die
is one of the issues that can crop up in science fiction,
where advances in medicine are extrapolated to a point
where death becomes optional. It is increasingly a moral
issue today. This ending does not leave us in any kind of
comfort zone.

There is no indication in the ending that Paolo's quest
has been anything other than a personal one. The wider
world he inhabits has not been improved by his actions.
Papa performs his distasteful functions with a musical

suppression of his residual emotions. He has the grace to stop singing when he sees the two observers but bows his head only because it is in the regulations to do so and he rounds off his duties with a great yawn.

We are not told who the two faceless watchers are. We think and hope that one of them is Paolo. We need to know that, as Vermont suggests, 'his sterk unbouin love for Nadia wid caw him throu' (p204). If one of the watchers is indeed Paolo, we cannot help wondering what his future will be. We would like to think that the two watchers are Paolo and Vermont. If we condense this book to a conflict of good and evil, they are the two representatives of good. In them we feel lies the last flicker of hope, but the book leaves us in a pessimistic 'fushionless Port nicht' (p207).

There are also elements of comedy in *But n Ben A-Go-Go*. The classical view of comedy involves the restoration of order in a world that has become disordered. Here we certainly have the disordered world and a small corner of it is put right. Such a definition of comedy is a very different thing from risible comedy, the kind of comedy that makes you laugh. There is certainly plenty of risible comedy in the novel. It is often said that laughter and tears are very close together and indeed in this novel they regularly share the same page.

It often spoils a joke to analyse it too deeply, but to discuss *But n Ben A-Go-Go* without making some mention of the range of humour it contains would be to do it an injustice. Some of the humour arises from incongruous and absurd images: transvestite Mongolian synchronised water ballet, or the idea of being disembowelled by the Empire State building, for example. A lot of the humour comes from wordplay like Portic Thistle and Submarnock. There is straightforward punning in the 'Eat and Greet Diner' (p57). Fitt has great fun combining Scots and foreign elements to give surprising new concepts like 'australian-rules shinty' (p118) and 'polis junks' (p89). The Scottish art of flyting produces insults like 'Ye're aboot as much use as solar panels on a mowdiewart's erse' (p34) which raise a few smiles as well.

For all the exuberant laughter in *But n Ben A-Go-Go*,

there is no rainbow promise of 'happy ever after' at the
end of this story. The floodwaters have not receded and
there is little to suggest the ultimate salvation of mankind.
Only now and again do flickers of hope appear. Two people
witness the committal of Nadia's body to the flames. We
wonder if hope resides in Paolo and Vermont. Also, in spite
of what the narrator tells us directly, Papa is not totally
unmoved by his task. When he started working at the
Medical Centre, he was deeply distressed and carries
indelible psychological scars from the days before he
learned to shut his mind off from the job. Even yet, the
reader can sense his horror at the feel of the corpse he is
removing. He has to make a conscious decision to empty his
mind. When he breaks with his usual practice and looks at
Nadia, although the narrator does not invite us to examine
Papa's emotions, we are left in no doubt that his need to
find a cheery tune is an antidote to atavistic feelings of
compassion and wistfulness. Now and again, throughout
the novel we catch glimpses of characters trying to subdue
their true feelings in order to present a stoic front and to
protect themselves from emotional involvement.

STRUCTURE

But n Ben-A-Go-Go is an extremely well structured novel, from the very first word of the novel, 'Moarnan', to the very last word, 'nicht'. This poetic detail alerts us to the fact that nothing in the writing of this book is haphazard. On the large scale there is an overall grand plan and on the smaller scale, not a word is wasted and all kinds of links are made between early and later chapters. We shall look at some of these towards the end of this section.

Fitt's novel is structured in several ways and on several levels and we will deal with each of these in turn. Its clever structuring and integrated storytelling make this a book which is just as good on a second reading or third reading. Even once you know the plot, it is a delight to see how you are led, and allowed to mislead yourself, along the way.

On first considering the structure of any text, it is a good idea just to flick through and see what catches the eye. What we see is a compact book, divided into chapters, with running chapter titles at the head of the right hand (recto) page and the running book title at the head of every left (verso) page. We also see that some pages are black with the type reversed out and there are some very distinctive introductory pages that look as though they really ought to be read. The introduction is in two parts.

Let us start at the very beginning with a quick word on introductions. Lots of people skip the introduction to a book. Only if the book merits further study might the student find an introduction attractive reading. *But n Ben A-Go-Go* is different. It is clear that the introduction is indeed an introduction from the Roman numerals at the foot of the page, but it manages to make itself look attractive by its unusual typographical features. It has a border and it is in a trendy font. It is a useful directive from the author on how to tackle his book. It is light, practical and informative and forecasts some of the wit that enriches the novel itself. We are ready to begin reading the novel with a curiosity to find and interpret new vocabulary and with all the essential background knowledge of place, time and society.

The other unusual typographical feature in the book is the use of black with the type reversed out in the pages from Nadia's kist. Visually, a barrier is created between these chapters and the rest. There is a barrier between Nadia and the rest of the world. We alone are privy to her thoughts as she lies within the physical barriers of the kist and her illness. Her thoughts are a source of dramatic irony, giving us information that the other characters do not have and in which the narrator has no place. It provides an interesting variation in the way information is presented. Here we have only the unvarnished and unedited thoughts of one character and we can judge her upon the innermost recesses of her mind, at a time when she is not presenting a public persona and can deceive no one but herself.

A flick through the recto page headers, or a glance at the contents page, will show that one of the chapters is the same name as the title of the book. What does this make you think? There are two strong strands to the story. The forward momentum of the narrative moves between Paolo and his father. Linking the strands together are Craw and Senga, both ubiquitous and insidious, the passive Nadia and the pro-active Vermont. The two parallel strands begin to come together at But n Ben A-Go-Go, and it seems that the climax of the novel is at hand, but when Paolo finally sees his father, it is the absent shell he sees. Diamond Broon's consciousness is in VINE and the actual meeting of father and son is postponed until the next chapter. The challenging of norms and expectations are part and parcel of this book, and if you were expecting a peak of tension in this chapter then you would have felt like a walker in the Scottish mountains who keeps expecting to see the summit over the next rise and finds there is always one more bit to climb. Just when you feel the tension is becoming unbearable, Fitt manages to string it out just a little longer.

Fitt uses all the tricks and techniques of creating suspense. Having more than one character to follow, he can leave one of them in a cliff-hanger situation and resume the storyline of another. He also gives us moments of relief, often underlined with humour, just so that we can be even more tortured by Paolo's next challenge or Diamond's next depravity. Right in the middle of the book, he seems to step right out of the story for a documentary on Hurricane Elvis. We understand the relevance to the plot, but it is highly unusual in that there is no reference in that entire chapter to any character who plays an active part in the plot. After that temporary respite, the plot, as they say, thickens. Vermont and Craw are stirred into the brew. The action speeds up and becomes even more intense before reaching a peak of tension and a final dénouement and the novel finishes with an epilogue. What are we to make of this playing with the ups and downs of our emotions? There is clearly nothing haphazard about the pacing of the narrative and within this larger roller-coaster structure there are all the structural supports that tie the novel together and give it a cohesiveness that you do not find in loosely planned and unpolished work. There are many such details. One of them is a pair of handcuffs with a pink fluffy lining. These Craw expects Vermont to wear while he gratifies his unnatural sexual desires. She refuses and Craw's response is swift and humiliating. It is her anger at his sexual bullying that makes her take a stand against him and ask for a decent assignment. At the end of the novel the handcuffs reappear as 'she sneckit his wrists wi the kitsch pink hauncuffs his men had left her in thon bleck nicht in her apartment on Elgin' (p204). Another example, this time from Nadia, is the name, Pavel, that she gives to her fantasy man in our first visit to her kist. In her last chapter, Tokyo Rose, she confuses Paolo with Pavel, thereby compounding her infidelities. Diamond Broon's connection with lugdrug is a third example. We are told that he is wrongly credited with inventing it. We are told that he was a DJ in Prag. It is not until much later that we are told that the drug is administered through the ear, to be taken with loud music. At that point the significance of the *lug* element of the name and the role a DJ could have in its use become explicit.

A lot of clues are planted in the course of the narrative which should indicate to the reader that all is not being revealed. When we are told that Broon will not be telling Sark the whole story (p50), we have no idea ourselves at that point what the whole story will be, and it is not until the second reading that we can really enjoy the irony of this remark. This is definitely a book that repays a second reading.

THEMES AND IMAGERY

Father and son

As in many Scottish novels, the relationship between father and son is explored. This relationship can be understood in a number of ways. There is a tension between the alpha male and the younger challenger. There is also a possible allusion to God the father. In the context of Calvinism as interpreted by the Klog family, this supposedly loving relationship is perverted into a need to control, just as Broon seeks to control Paolo, even to the extent of ordaining his death. The relationship of the state and the citizen is similarly one of parental control. The importance of this family relationship is underlined by the centrality of DNA to the plot.

DNA

DNA is a symbol which pervades the novel. DNA is the basis of life. Paradoxically, in this novel it is the means by which Nadia can be allowed to die. Hence, it is the object of Paolo's quest, the search for the DNA which will free Nadia, the bringer of death. As the giver of life, it is the source of inherited characteristics; it is the chemical structure which determines not just physical qualities, but also behavioural propensities. Both of these are affected by what we eat, how we train, what we learn and the experiences we have, but the raw material that we have to work on is, essentially, the product of our DNA and the balance between nature and nurture is a recurring theme in the novel. Our first introduction to Paolo draws our attention instantly to his genetic make-up on his mother's side and there are reminders of his maternal genes at frequent intervals. At the climax of the novel, it is the similarity between his DNA and his father's DNA that allows us to believe in the horrific concept of Direct Organ Transplant and provides the rationale for his father's actions. Paolo needs to know what of his father there is in himself. There is even a case for likening the structure of the novel itself to the double helix of DNA as we see the manoeuvring of Diamond and the journey of Paolo as two

longitudinal strands linked throughout their length by the
cross strands of Nadia, Vermont, Sark and Senga, two
parallel quests, for the DNA of the father and for the DNA
of the son, one good, one evil, twisting and turning together
throughout the book. The last time we meet Nadia, she
describes herself as 'a soonless, enless spiral' (p140), an
echo of the DNA molecule.

The sun
The sun is presented in the novel as a source of danger
and pain. It is inescapable and vicious. This turns on its
head our usual idea of the sun being a symbol of life, of
pleasant warmth and comfort, a source of light that chases
away the fears and evils of darkness. We are accustomed to
thinking of the sun as a symbol of all that is good. We are
also accustomed to thinking of the sun as a symbol of the
expected course of the seasons. It comes as a shock to read
in the world of 2090 that the sun in January, in the latitude
of Scotland, is unbearably hot. This reinforces our impression of an alien, unfamilar and unsettled world. Still,
the idea of light being good and darkness being associated
with evil dies hard. The Café o the Twa Suns (named after
the house of the Czech writer and poet, Jan Neruda, author
of *Tales of the Malá Strana*) relies on traditional sun
imagery. Of the two suns above the door, we are told 'sic a
kenmerk hotched wi irony. Atween them, the puir wee suns
couldna manage even a caunle's worth of licht, no when
the double gloaman o Sark an Broon cast its soor shaddas
owre the truth' (p179-80). There remains, however a sense
that Diamond Broon and Sark are themselves two suns,
powerful, harsh, brilliant and relentless, a pair of evil sun
gods, inverting the expected values of fatherhood,
friendship and duty. This thought occurs to Vermont as she
tends to Paolo and sees the dying Diamond and the
handcuffed, humiliated Craw: 'Twa suns, she thought, spent
efter their final gloaman' (p204).

The rose
The rose is a universal symbol of love. The bonsai rose in
But n Ben A-Go-Go is, like much of the rest of the

symbolism in this book, ambiguous and warped. For one thing, this rose is not the traditional red one. Our first thought is that it is indeed a simple love token, brought by Paolo to the woman he loves. This misconception is soon put right by the association with Tokyo Rose and betrayal. Any thought that its appearance on Nadia's thought screen might have been a simple confession is quickly dispersed with the knowledge that she is in the kist because she had sex with another man. Therefore, Paolo must have known about her betrayal as soon as she was kisted. Why then does she project that image? Paolo thinks she is taunting him, but the true answer must be deduced from Nadia's character with the further knowledge which we and Paolo become party to later, that she was first given a bonsai rose by the person with whom she betrayed Paolo, Diamond Broon himself. It is not until he has this information that Paolo realises Nadia was giving a clue to her lover's identity. We discover that Diamond Broon gives a similar rose to all his many sexual partners. For Diamond, the rose represents not love but the beauty, delicacy and youth that he takes and destroys. We learn from him that these roses are not grown in the traditional manner but are mass produced by hydroponics in a greenhouse. Somehow this seems to further distort the symbolism of a lover's gift of a single rose.

The flood

It is impossible not to draw parallels with the flood described in the *Old Testament* which tells us how God sent a flood to destroy people because their wickedness displeased him. In fact, it is explicitly referred to as 'God's flood'. The obvious implication is that the flood is a punishment for mankind's folly. It is difficult to sustain an analogy with the biblical flood much further than that, however. In Fitt's flood, the survivors are not the good and deserving Noah and his family. They are hard-bitten pragmatists surviving in a materialistic, post-religious world. The waters are still high and there is no olive branch in sight.

VINE
It could be said that virtual reality is a metaphor for the suspension of disbelief that attends the reading of a good novel. We become so immersed in the story that we feel we are actually there. Just as in the book the edges between RealTime and VINE are blurred, so we are aware that there is truth in the fiction. We see the reflection of our own society. We have a glimpse into the future of society. We witness the strength of love and the depths of depravity and we are conscious of the continuing battle between good and evil. All these are truths set in a fantasy world of superhero, arch-villains and improbable technologies.

SUGGESTED WORKS FOR COMPARISON

There are several aspects of *But n Ben A-Go-Go* which deserve to be seen in the context of other works of literature and which provide interesting comparisons and contrasts.

But n Ben A-Go-Go, The Time Machine by H. G. Wells and *Nineteen Eighty-Four* by George Orwell are a trio begging for comparison. They are obviously linked by the science fiction genre, although it should be noted that the phrase 'science fiction' had not even been invented when Wells was writing, even if he is often described as the father of the form. The three novels look at different periods. *The Time Machine* carries us into the far future of 802,701 and beyond, while Orwell's date of 1984 has already passed. Fitt's choice of 2090 is more on the Orwellian scale than the Wellsian. The language of the three novels is very different. For one thing, *The Time Machine* and *Nineteen Eighty-Four* are in English, but that is not all there is to say. The gentlemanly late Victorian prose of Wells is very different in its vocabulary and sentence construction from Orwell's short sentences and lively dialogue. Like Fitt, Orwell creates a new vocabulary for his future world. The structure of this *Newspeak* language is explained by Orwell in an appendix to the novel and from this we can see his use of affixation, compounding and clipping as means of word-formation to give such creations as *doublepluscold, prolefeed, Minipax, thinkpol* and so on. Like Fitt, Orwell was very conscious of the power of language but, while Fitt celebrates and expands the language of the future, Orwell pictures its diminution as a means of communication and illustrates instead its role as an instrument of propaganda and manipulation of thought.

The manner of narration is also worthy of comparison. In *The Time Machine* a first person narrator appears as a character, on an equal footing with other characters in the novel, struggling to understand events that are beyond his ken. In the course of the novel, he hands over to another character, while he himself sits back and listens. When the Time Traveller finishes his story, the narration is taken up

again by the first voice, commenting on the reaction of the
other characters to what they have heard and concluding
the novel. In *Nineteen Eighty-Four*, an omniscient first person
narrator describes, comments and analyses at great length.
In *But n Ben A-Go-Go*, there is comparatively little description or explanation from the narrator, and almost no
analysis. We are left to make up our own minds. Apart from
the lull in the action in chapter 11, the narrator plays a
minimal role other than as an impartial describer of action,
as a way of seeing through the eyes of the characters and
as a link between speakers.

As well as these areas of comparison, which could be
expounded at much greater length, there are one or two
individual but very significant similarities between *But n
Ben A-Go-Go* and *The Time Machine*. In *The Time Machine*,
mankind has become divided into two separate species, the
Eloi, who live above ground, and the pallid, blond, sub-
terranean *Morlocks* with large eyes, who cannot bear the
light. This is an extreme division but in Fitt's 2090, there
are already sun-tolerant *melanos* and pale skinned sun-
intolerant *albinos*. The comparison goes no further than
that because in *But n Ben A-Go-Go* there is no hint of a
social or behavioural divide on the grounds of skin colour
or tolerance to light. Another superficial but interesting
point of comparison is the global temperature. In the year
802,701, the temperature is higher than it is now. Wells does
not attribute this to the same causes as we do today. His
reasons were that the planets are moving closer to the sun.
Nevertheless, it is curious that global warming spans the
two novels written over a century apart. A further comparison could be drawn between Big Brother and Ceilidh,
both of whom have oppressive powers of surveillance. The
CCTV cameras, tags and sensors are everywhere.

Other texts that could be studied in conjunction with
But n Ben A-Go-Go might include one of Ian Fleming's
James Bond novels and one of Ian Rankin's Inspector Rebus
detective novels. Such comparisons could be used to throw
light on the techniques of drawing a convincing, rounded
character. In Inspector Rebus, we have gritty realism
and a character who is not easy to like, but we are drawn

to him because he is vulnerable and we can empathise with him and his very human failings. James Bond is just too smooth. We know he is going to come through amazing dangers without a hair out of place. Paolo is a combination of vulnerable cyberjanny and superhero. Rankin, Fleming and Fitt also bear comparison in their ability to construct an exciting plot and to keep the reader guessing.

Another Scottish writer of science fiction is Iain M Banks. His style is very different from that of Matthew Fitt, but one of his books, written as Iain Banks (his non-science fiction persona), affords a useful comparison and contrast with *But n Ben A-Go-Go* on a number of points, including location, the nature of reality, structure and the use of leitmotifs. This is a novel called *The Bridge*. As the cover illustration suggests, the bridge in question is the Forth Rail Bridge. Like Fitt, Banks used a distorted version of a topography with which the reader is conversant, playing on familiar names and familiar references. Although we are not told initially that the Forth Bridge is indeed the location in which the novel is set, we gather that the bridge of the title joins the City and the Kingdom. We assume that this refers to the City of Edinburgh and the Kingdom of Fife. The pattern of the girders confirms this suspicion, but the bridge that the central character inhabits for much of the novel is a strange and surreal place.

The Bridge opens with a short, fragmented, tortured stream of consciousness, not unlike the musings of Nadia. We are then treated to an unsettling series of shifts in our perceptions of reality, which we eventually come to reconsider as levels of consciousness. The second chapter is dream-like in its irrationality and then we discover that it is indeed being recounted as a dream. Then, just as we think we are beginning to understand what is going on, we find out that the dream itself is a fiction created by the main character intended to deceive his psychiatrist. As in *But n Ben A-Go-Go*, levels of consciousness and out-of-body experience are explored. Indeed, the activity of the mind independent of the physical body is essential to both novels but, while Fitt uses VINE to advance the plot, Banks uses the activity of the mind much more as an end in itself. For

him, the plot is itself the Kafkaesque, erratic journey of
the mind back to reality. Both books, however, move
between different states of consciousness.

Just as *But n Ben A-Go-Go* has its leitmotifs of the sun,
the bonsai rose and so on, *The Bridge* has the protagonist's
circular pain in the chest and the hospital scene on the TV
screen, etc. In both novels, these devices help to give
cohesion throughout. In the case of *But n Ben A-Go-Go*,
they cement an already very tight structure, held together
by a rapidly advancing plot and a journey towards a known
goal. In the case of *The Bridge*, these motifs are needed to
stabilise an amorphous and unstable plot where a journey
has been suspended. Perhaps the best point of comparison
between the two novels is the talent that both authors have
for combining hilarious wit with great sadness and
poignancy.

For the serious student of Scots, it would be of interest
to make a comparison of *But n Ben A-Go-Go* with Scots of
an earlier period or Modern Scots approached in a different
way.

A poignant tale of betrayed love from Older Scots would
be Henryson's *Testament of Cresseid*. This continues the story
set during the Trojan war. Chaucer wrote of Cresseid's
betrayal of Troilus with Diomede and of her defection to the
Greek camp where she became a common whore. Henryson
takes up the tale where Cresseid, goes back to her father
and blames Cupid for her misfortunes. She dreams that the
Gods punish her for her disrespect by inflicting the disease
of leprosy on her. However the contemporary reader would
know that leprosy was regarded as a punishment for
inappropriate sexual exploits. She suffers the exile that was
meted out to lepers. The similarities so far between
Cresseid and Nadia are considerable. However, Troilus, her
first love, reacts to something in her and gives her alms
but does not recognise her. She repents deeply and learns
from her mistake.

The language is in a courtly style with many Latinate
and French borrowings, but there is still a lot of easily
recognisable Scots vocabulary. Like *But n Ben A-Go-Go* the
trick is to read it aloud if it seems hard to understand at

first. It is interesting to see in this older text where some of the Modern Scots spellings and morphological features come from.

The obvious choice for comparison from Modern Scots would be one of the novels of Irvine Welsh, such as *Trainspotting*. There is nothing courtly about this style. The spellings here are interesting in a different way, in that they reflect the pronunciation of informal speech in a certain sub-class of Leith. There is a lot of very interesting vocabulary which can be discussed in the same structured manner as was used above for the vocabulary of *But n Ben A-Go-Go*.

Other literary and linguistic comparisons that could be made with *But n Ben A-Go-Go* include an examination of the representation of women. Nadia and Vermont could be compared and contrasted with Henryson's Cresseid or with other female figures in Scottish literature such as Chris Guthrie in *A Scots Quair*. This last would provide a wealth of material for discussion on the linguistic front as well, not just in terms of the Kincardineshire dialect but in the way in which Scots is represented on the page.

FITT'S CREATIVE USE OF LANGUAGE

One of the first things to strike the reader is that this book
is written in Scots. Some advice entitled 'How to read *But
n Ben A-Go Go*' prefaces the book and gives realistic
insights into the status of Scots today as well as providing
practical tips on reading Scots. In explaining how to deduce
the meaning of new word formations such as *incendicowp*,
it reminds the reader of the process of deriving meaning
from context in a way that all students who have ever done
an interpretation exercise should be familiar with. There
are a lot of words in the book that are bound to be
unfamiliar but most young readers expand their vocabulary
with every book they read, whatever the language. Readers
who take their teachers' advice and read with a dictionary
at their elbow might like to substitute a good Scots
dictionary, such as the *Concise Scots Dictionary*, for their
usual volume, but most readers will soon become too
absorbed in the story to consult works of reference.
Working out the meaning of new words is part of the fun of
this book, and the science fiction genre means that many
of the neologisms are not in the dictionary anyway – at
least, not yet!

The sight of the words may be unfamiliar but the
sounds are those that Scots hear every day. So, if a
sentence is a bit difficult at first, read it aloud and listen
to it. In fact, hearing the words in your head as you read
is a particular joy in this book. Just as if it were a well
cast radio play, each character has a distinctive voice and
Fitt uses different regional accents of Scots to help achieve
this.

Matthew Fitt is doing something so rational, so normal,
that all Scots speakers should be asking why it has not
been done before. He is simply writing in Scots, not with a
self-conscious switching between English and Scots, but in
natural language. There is no artificial and curious
linguistic divide. Where the characters and the readers are
Scots speakers, it is absurd to tell a story through the
medium of an English authorial voice. Fitt has identified
this absurdity and done something about it.

Vocabulary

The first and perhaps most obvious feature of Fitt's language is the vocabulary. The science fiction genre and the cultural mix that is such a feature of this novel would open the door to innovative vocabulary in any language. For the moment, we are concerned with the vocabulary features that are distinctively Scots. Many words in the book are shared by both Scots and English although some of these like *throu, roch, gless, stane* and so on may have a slightly different form. You can easily deduce the English words that these correspond to. In the case of *throu*, the only real difference is one of spelling, the omission of *gh* being a rationalisation of the spelling, recognising the loss of a final consonant which has not been pronounced in SBrE (South British Standard English) since the end of the sixteenth century. Scots, however retains this final consonant in *roch* (which rhymes with *loch*). The same consonant has become [f] in English *rough*. (Here and in what follows, square brackets enclose symbols used in the International Phonetic Alphabet, a system used by linguists throughout the world to represent sounds on a page as accurately as possible. The meaning of the symbols used here are self-evident but, if you want to know more, see McMahon, 2002.)

Again, in Scots the spelling has been rationalised because Scots tend to read *gh* with their 'English-reading eyes', whereas they read *ch* with their 'Scots-reading eyes'. *Stane* looks more like *stân*, the Old English word that it derives from than the modern English form, although the pronunciation has changed in both cases. *Bleck* and *black* are obviously cognates, as are *gless* and *glass*, *tap* and *top*, *braid* and *broad*, *lang* and *long*, *doon* and *down*, *strong* and *strang* and so on. You may even see some regular patterns emerging if you compare enough Scots-English pairs.

Sometimes Scots is conservative and retains Old English words which have been lost from SBrE, like *kythe, oxter, thole* and *smeddum*.

Old English words are the first layer of vocabulary in both English and Scots on which everything else is overlaid, and much of the overlaying shows evidence of the

other languages with which we came into contact, reflecting our military, political and commercial past.

There are quite a few Old Norse loan words here dating
all the way back to the period of the Danish Vikings.
Again, some of these have spread southwards from the
Danelaw and made their way into SBrE and SSE (Standard
Scottish English) as well as Scots. *Sky* is one of these. The
Old English word was *lift*, still found in Scots and poetic
English (cf German *luft*). *Skin* is another. The Old English
word was *fell*. *Baith* is an Old Norse loan which survives in
English as *both*. These everyday loans serve to illustrate
just how deeply Old Norse penetrated into English and
Scots. *Blether*, *kist* and *skited* are further examples of Old
Norse words in Scots.

We also find loan words from Gaelic. Obviously the
place-name *Cúl Mor* is Gaelic and has not been naturalised
as a Scots vocabulary item, but *glen* is a word known to
everyone in Scotland as a Scots word.

There are Dutch words, as you would expect from the
history of Scots, including *haar*, *redd* and *gowf*. *Plot*, in
the sense it is used here, also comes from Dutch.

If you speak a little French, take a moment to scan
through the first two pages of chapter three and see which
words strike you as being French loan words. Some of the
earlier French loan words have been around in Scots for so
long that they have become completely naturalised and
you may not even notice that they are French in origin.
Centre, *prison*, *gaird* and *rich* might come into this category.
Other words such as *entourage*, *chef* and *regime*, are much
later loans. Although fully absorbed into Scots, they still
retain a faint hint of their origins in that their spelling does
not match their pronunciation, if Scots (or English) spelling
conventions are applied.

There are some other words that you may feel are a bit
too modern or learned-looking to have come from Old
English. They may also have come from French. The
problem is that French is descended from Latin and it is
sometimes quite difficult to know without looking up a
dictionary whether a word was borrowed into Scots or
English via French or directly from Latin. Such words in

this text are *command, ocean* and *cylinder. Solar, penitentiary* and *maximum* probably do come directly from Latin.

With this tradition of borrowing already in the language, Scots is open to continued borrowing from other languages and here we find a large number of modern loans from a variety of languages all contributing to the international mix of the world that Fitt creates. Again, even within the limited space of the opening pages of chapter three we find such loans include *adobe* from Spanish, *gneiss* from German, *diaquiri* after a Cuban village, and *piazza* from Italian. This rich history of the language allows Fitt to make extravagant use of borrowing throughout *But n Ben A-Go-Go* to give a sense of cultural diversity.

These examples above represent the range of sources of Scots vocabulary that Fitt has ready access to, but he goes beyond the existing lexicon of Scots and extends it by using existing words in new contexts, stretching their meanings to accommodate new uses. He also uses a common method of expanding the lexicon known as conversion. This simply means using a word that belongs to a particular word class as if it belonged to another. An example of this that will be familiar to you is *text*. Until recently *text* was a noun. Now it can also be used as a verb, *to text*. Examples in the novel are *oxter* (p13), and *pairty* (p205) which started off as nouns but which are used here as verbs, and *coorie* (p203) a noun formed from a verb.

The methods of expanding the vocabulary that were most popular with the Anglo-Saxons were compounding and affixation, and Fitt makes full use of these. Compounding means joining two or more roots together to make a new word and it is one of Fitt's favourite ways of satisfying his need for words to describe the new and as yet unnamed concepts in his world of the future, like *germsooker* (p5). He also uses compounding to create Scots alternatives to existing words such as *clood-kittler* (p10) for 'skyscraper'. An alternative Scots word *skyscarter* (p11) has been in use for some time. It is what is known as a calque, or loan-translation. Again this is a process of word formation which has been around in Scots and English for a very long time. For example, we have the word *cut-throat* as a direct translation of the French *coupe-gorge*. So in *But n Ben A-Go-Go*, by translation of all or part of an English word, 'plastic bag' becomes *plastipoke* (p5); 'world-famous' becomes *world-kenspeckle* (p21) and a 'ground to air' missile is a *yird-til-lift* one (p55).

Affixation is another kind of word formation that was favoured by the Anglo-Saxons. Prefixes and suffixes can be used to create new words. Fitt uses many existing examples and provides a few more of his own, sometimes using distinctively Scots affixes in the process. *Smeerich* has the Scots diminutive suffix *-ich*. The prefix *a-*, common to both English and Scots, is used much more widely in Scots, often in contexts where English would have *be-*. So we find *ahint* (p145), *atween* (p145) and *afore* (p147). Another prefix common to both is *mis-*, which carries the sense of 'wrongly'. This is more productive in Scots and gives words like *misken* (p29). *Toomness* takes the Scots root *toom* and adds a suffix *-ness* common to both English and Scots. In *circumpauchle*, the latinate prefix *circum-* is added to a Scots root.

If readers find his new words attractive and useful and if, as a result, their use of these words becomes widespread, we can look forward to the words appearing in dictionaries in the future.

Spelling

One of the problems of writing in Scots, or one of the freedoms, depending on your point of view, is the lack of uniformity in Scots spelling. Spelling has not always been fixed in English either. Chaucer and Shakespeare had plenty of inconsistencies in their spelling and if they wanted to write a word they didn't know how to spell, they just wrote down what the word sounded like. Nobody complained until the late fifteenth century when people began to notice that pronunciation was changing and spelling and pronunciation were getting out of step. By the sixteenth and seventeenth century, a lot had been written about spelling reform and the people who were describing their new spelling systems provided invaluable evidence about the way language was developing, even if nobody except other spelling reformers paid much notice to their sometimes ingenious suggestions at the time. By the eighteenth century, people had begun compiling English dictionaries and that was just at the time when Scots went into a disastrous decline as a medium for formal writing. This meant that there was a lack of prestigious models for how Scots should be written down. As English became increasingly standardised, Scots became increasingly fragmented and, of its many dialects, no single dialect emerged as a standard and so no single spelling system can claim superiority. Fitt uses a lot of commonsense along with his own knowledge as a native speaker of Scots to produce a spelling system which makes his intention very clear to other Scots speakers without alienating readers who are not accustomed to reading Scots.

Some regular pronunciation differences reflected in the spelling

If we look at words like *hae, doo, o* and *siller*, we can see that they have something in common. They have all lost a [v]. Put it back in and there we have the English *have, dove, of* and *silver*. L-vocalisation is another feature that is common in Scots. The evidence for L-vocalisation in *But n Ben-A-Go-Go* is found in words like *pou*. The English cognate of this is *pull*. In some accents of Scots, the [l] remains but *pull* rhymes with *dull*. This set of words in Scots provides a good example of lexical diffusion. L-vocalisation is a change in progress and it affects some words sooner than others. No Scot would as yet drop the [l] from *bull*. *Aw* or *aa* (all), *haud* (hold) and *baws* or *baas* (balls) provide further examples where the change takes place. *Saw* (salve) in 'MDZ peels sawed the pain' (p15) shows both v-deletion and L-vocalisation.

The reason why this feature is called l-vocalisation is that the [l] does not just disappear; it becomes a vowel and then, if there is a vowel next to it, it will merge into that vowel. What happens is that Scots make their [l] sounds with the back of their tongues raised and their tongues touching the alveolar ridge just behind the teeth. Among other sounds Scots make with the back of the tongue raised are [w], the glottal stop and the [o] vowel as in *code*. If you listen to a Scots speaker, especially one from the Central Belt, that uses the glottal stop in words like *little* and *bottle*, you will hear the [l] losing the articulation between the tip of the tongue and the alveolar ridge and what you actually hear is more like an [o]. This is L-vocalisation in action, especially following a glottal stop.

TH-deletion is evidenced in *wi* (with), *claes* (clothes) and *smoor* (smother) where the [θ] sound (as in *thigh*) and [đ] sounds (as in *thy*) are lost. We also find the spelling *hink* (think) (p9). This [h] substitution for [θ] is a feature of informal Scots.

Speakers tend to be a bit lazy. Listen to the way people pronounce *factsheet*. Hardly anyone puts a [t] in the middle. Simplification of consonants clusters is not exclusive to Scots and it has being going on for a long time, as spellings such as *gnash* and *knife* suggest. There are, however, some Scots examples that occur very frequently. Consider the following words: *roon, haun, staun*. In each case the [nd] cluster has undergone simplification with the loss of [d]. If you try to feel what your mouth is doing when you say [n] and [d], you should be able to feel that they are both made with the tip of the tongue on the alveolar ridge, behind the top teeth. Where two consonants that are made in the same place come together, it is quite common for one to be lost. A similar thing happens in *nummer*. Again, take a moment to think and feel where the [m] sound and the [b] sound are made. This time, they are both made by the lips and the [b] in *number* is lost, just as in English *lamb* and *comb*.

A good example of how Fitt uses non-standard spelling to suggest pronunciation is *ackually* (p152) where a [kt] cluster has been simplified. Note that this is not the same thing that causes the difference between Scots and English in present participle and verbal noun endings. Listen to the English *-ing* ending. There is no [g] there at all. It is a single [ŋ] sound. So when we compare Scots *shoppin* with English *shopping*, it is a nonsense to talk about simplification of a consonant cluster, or loss of [g], since there is none there to lose.

Accurate reflection of Scots grammar

There is more to Scots than just the vocabulary, the pronunciation and the spelling. Just replacing English words with Scots ones does not give you Scots. There are a number of differences between the two languages in the grammar as well.

Pronouns: *Mines* is used for the possessive when it is not followed by the noun it refers to. *Ah'll gie ye a shot o mines.* (p200).This regularises the morphology since it now works like *yours, ours, hers* and *theirs.*

The reflexive pronouns also show more regularity than in English, consisting of the possessive personal pronoun plus *-sel* in the singular and *-sels* in the plural. So *hissel* and *theirsels* conform to the pattern, whereas in English *himself* and *themselves* create irregularities.

Verb: These show even more differences from SBrE. In the present tense, it is not uncommon to have what looks like a singular verb with a plural subject:

> *... paradoxes wis whit the Diamond wis aw aboot* (p188).
> *The streets is toom ...* (p52).

This historically happened only if the subject is not an adjacent personal pronoun and that is why this kind of occurrence is sometimes said to obey the Northern Personal Pronoun Rule. It is also found in Northern dialects of English.

The present participle and the verbal noun (often called the gerund) are formed in Scots by adding *-in*. Examples of the present participle as part of a verb group include *the mowdie inside him wis stertin tae nip* (p7) and *they were soon jiggin tae a different tune* (p11).

Verbal nouns are exemplified by *shoppin* in *lowsed by the lord fae prozac, sex and involuntary hame shoppin* (p 4).

Past tenses and past participles in Scots often differ from the past tenses and past participles of their English cognates. One obvious and common difference is the use of *-t* or *-it* where English would use *-ed* in weak verbs. Most

Scots use a mixture of *-it* and *-ed* endings and Matthew Fitt
is no exception. Thus we find *gart, confrontit* and *slippit*
alongside *bosied, beardied, havered, kisted* and *kittled* (p4).
The majority of verbs in English and Scots are weak verbs,
so much so that they are often referred to as regular
verbs – although historically, and even today, definite
regular patterns can also be discerned in the morphology of
the strong verbs, those which change their internal vowel
to show tense. Speakers of Scots and English really can't be
bothered with too much inflectional morphology and what
has happened over the years is that we have gradually
simplified and 'regularised' it. For this to happen, a number
of verbs that used to be strong verbs have become weak,
but the verbs that have made this transition in Scots are
not necessarily the same as the ones that have done it in
English. *Swim* is a strong verb in English but in *But n Ben
A-Go-Go*, its cognate is a weak verb *soom* with its past tense
and past participle appearing as *soomed* (p177). Another
examples is *growed* (p204). The same applies to *faaed*, the
weak past tense of *faa*, the L-vocalised cognate of the strong
English verb *fall*. Another way of simplifying verb morphology in the strong verbs is to make the past tense the
same as the past participle. Instead of *swim* having a past
tense of *swam* and the past participle *swum*, younger
speakers are increasingly using *swum* for both. It has
already happened with *sting* in English where the part
tense and the past participle are both *stung*, but Scots
retains *stang* in the past tense: *the thocht o the satellites
stravaigin the earth's orbit abinn stang him on.* An
interesting example of Scots being more conservative than
English in this respect is in the verb *hae*. In English, *have*
has both the past tense and the past participle *had*. Fitt
retains a difference with the past tense *had* and the past
participle *haen*. The *-en* is an inflectional ending which
was frequently attached to past participles, cf *give gave given*;
drive drove driven. (*Have* also shows v-deletion in both
Scots and English, since *have+-ed* becomes *had* in English.
However, we find a counter example in *His keffiyah wis
tore* (p133), where English retains the *-en* inflection in the
form *torn.*

From this is it abundantly clear that both Scots and English are in a state of flux. Scots, because it has escaped the constraints of prescriptive grammar teachers, shows a greater variation and this creates a climate for change. No living language is set in stone. These changes are taking place all around us and, while English teachers and language conservationists may throw up their hands in horror, many of these collapses of past tenses with past participles will become so much part of everyday language that the grammar books will eventually have to be re-written. Ongoing changes produce such controversial utterances as *I seen, I done and I have went.* When Fitt uses *he seen* (p136) many Scots purists are likely to be up in arms, but Fitt at least has the defence that this is a sci-fi novel and these look like being the verb forms of the future.

Syntax: A feature of Scots syntax, or word order, that comes from contact with Gaelic is the positioning of the participle at the end in constructions like *his hert wis a lowe o hate become* (p45) or *The western sky wis a dour colour turnin* (p147).

In some regions of Scotland, you will hear a double modal verb as in *I'll no can thole that tae happen* (p202). In SSE and SBrE you may have the *will* or the *can*, but not both.

Individual voices

The novel is written in a variety of Scots that is compatible with speech across a wide swathe of central Scotland. Certain characters, though, have distinctive voices and this is used for dramatic effect.

Java 5 speaks in Dundee dialect. The main feature of this is to pronounce the vowel that SSE speakers have in the pronoun *I* as if it were *Eh*. What is most interesting is that Dundonians do change the diphthong into a monophthong in all words. It only happens regularly before

- the final sounds in the words *hive writhe rise*
- [r]
- certain syllable boundaries.

So, in Dundonian, *five* becomes *fehve* and *rise* becomes *rehz* but *Fife* is still *Fife* and *rice* is still *rice*. Java 5 uses *Eh* as its first person pronoun. Other examples are *onyweh* (p35), *trehin* (p35), *hypnotehsed* (p177) and *fehve* (p178). Another marker of the Dundonian accent of Java 5 is an *a* sound where West and Central Scotland would use *aw*. So in Java 5's accent *braw* becomes *bra* (p34). His pronunciation of *auld* is represented as *aald*.

Certainly the most effective use of dialect in the book is the North-East speech of the character, Sark. Fitt cheats just a little bit when we first meet the owner of this particular voice by giving us only a few clues to his origins. There is little of the Doric in the first utterances of Sark, but there are one or two important clues. As in Dundonian, the pronunciation of *auld* is most closely represented by *aald* and *aw* is represented as *aa*, but the most salient feature, the one that really gives this speaker away as a north-east speaker is the substitution of [f] for the sound usually represented in spelling by *wh* and pronounced by most Scots as [hw]. Sark asks Paolo, 'Ye ken fit it means?' (p82) As if to draw our attention to the differences, Paolo repeats, 'Ah ken fine whit it means, auld man.' It is easy enough to spot on the second reading, but Fitt's brushstrokes are so light that on a first reading of the book, a reader caught up in the excitement of the story might easily miss these clues.

The North-East accent is much more evident when we meet Craw. In addition to the substitution of [f] for [hw], we find the highly distinctive *gweed* representing the word which appears elsewhere in the text as *guid*. *Aince* appears as *eence*, *brawest* as *braaest*. There are also vocabulary items associated with the North-East, such as *quine* and *loun*. We are in no doubt as to the origins of Craw. We will recognise this voice when we hear it again, chillingly, in Chapter 22: 'Fit div ye think ye're daein, quinie?' (p196) There is absolutely no doubt that this moment is one of the highlights of the book.

The underplaying of Sark's accent is necessary in order to surprise us when we discover that Sark is Craw but, when we go back and check on Sark's earlier utterances, there is enough there to allow us to believe that Sark and Craw speak with one and the same voice.

Stylistics

A branch of language study which is particularly useful to students of literature is stylistics. Through this systematic study of the way language is used, we can arrive at a much deeper understanding of a text, of the effects it creates and of the techniques the writer is using to create these effects. In *But n Ben A-Go-Go* the individual characters have very different voices and we have looked at some of the differences in Sociolinguistics and Regional Variation. These along with all the other language topics introduced in this *Scotnote* feed into a stylistic analysis of the text.

We have already remarked on the graphology of p1 and how it separates off Nadia's sections from the rest of the text, just as she herself is cut off from the world. The chapter heading looks a little like the standing information on a screen. It is as if we are reading her thought screen. The grammar is unusual in that there are a lot of sentence fragments. The first words of Nadia are the first words of the book. Apart from the title, we have as yet no clues to work from. Her first word, 'Moarnan', could be a greeting or it could merely be an indication of the time of day. The next utterance is not a well-formed sentence. There is no subject and no main verb. 'I am' is omitted. The second utterance is also lacking a subject. The third and fourth lack a finite verb. In fact, there is only one complete sentence in that paragraph. This creates the impression of private thoughts, not prose that has been constructed for someone else to read. The way in which *the* is used shows that the point of view is not that of an impartial observer. Unless a *the* refers to some universal known like 'the world' or 'the sky' or 'the truth', *the* is not used with a noun that has not been previously introduced. *The* usually refers backwards. There has been no previous reference to *the porters*. The reader does not know which porters are being referred to and so this knowledge must be in the head of the speaker (or, in this case, the thinker). The reader soon realises that this is a stream of consciousness, but it is the

writer's use of syntax that creates this effect. The short paragraphs, separated by *oot* give the impression of short bursts
of mental activity. As more of the nature of Nadia's
condition is revealed, this is seen to be realistic. As the
chapter proceeds, the *oot* of a radio communication gives
way to single words which seem to represent a pause, a
hitch in the thought processes, again suggesting fragmentation of thought.

Names
One of the ways that linguists use to trace the history of
languages and the movements of the people who speak them
is through onomastics, the study of place and personal
names.

One of the advantages of setting the novel in the not
too distant future is the scope for playing with names.
When we are in the middle of history being made, it is
impossible to know how future generations will record it.
As they say, 'anyone who can remember the 60s wasn't
really there'. Fitt allows himself the luxury of looking
backwards with the eyes of the future, editing history.
Nelson Mandela has already given his name to streets and
squares. Who knows what other names will become
landmarks? Appropriately, Fitt selects a great musical
figure of the late twentieth century and early twenty-first
century to commemorate in the naming of the *Evelyn Glennie
Music Faculty*. Falkirk is the site of the *John MacLean
International Airport*. This is a powerful affirmation of
Scotland's political past, putting John MacLean alongside
Charles de Gaulle and John F. Kennedy (now situated in
New Appalachia, wherever that may be) as a name for an
International Airport. *Lorne Gillies Square*, appropriately in
the Gaelic Quarter on Dumfries is named for the renowned
Gaelic singer, Anne Lorne Gillies. A chain of newsagents
and stationers which has only recently disappeared from
our High Streets is recalled in the name *Jeremiah Menzies*
on a plastic bag and Doc Marten is promoted to professor.
This blurring of reality and fantasy assists in maintaining
the continuity of present and future whilst unsettling us

with a knowledge of the otherness of 2090. It is also a source of gentle humour and wit.

Less gently, there is a biting sense of irony in the naming of the timeshare penitentiaries to suggest theme parks: *Inverdisney*, *Disney Alp* and *Lake Walt*. This irony is doubled by the fact that VINE, the virtual reality where Diamond Broon feels most free, is much more of an unreal, theme park experience.

Names like *Submarnock* for the undersea prison and *Portic Thistle* FC *and dundonese man-o-war are just plain good fun.*

Names have been changed, perhaps reflecting changes in the landscape but also making them more international and so the Irish sea has become the *Irish Skagerrak* and Schiehallion has lost its Celtic name and gone from being the seat of the Caledonian fairies to become the blandly labelled *Massimo 7*. The world is shrinking. Even today, phrases like 'global village' are commonplace.

Fitt makes the most of this in place names and personal names. The Danes live in *Favela Copenhagen*. Broon's Inuit sidekick, Sawney Ip, has the same first name as the legendary family of Scottish cannibals. Dr Hans Cairns has a Germanic first name and a Celtic surname. Paolo Stevenson Broon himself sounds quite international.

Conclusion

For the non-Scots reader, the language of *But n Ben A-Go-Go* is undoubtedly hard work. Even for the Scots reader, it is full of surprises and challenges. Very few Scots use their language as densely as Fitt does in this novel; most Scots speakers dilute their language with varying quantities of English depending on the situation. The widely accepted prestige language of Scotland is Scottish Standard English, the language of education and the perceived language of authority. The narrator of a novel, as an authority figure, often omniscient and usually to be trusted, is therefore expected to speak English. Fitt challenges this convention and, in so doing, highlights the irrationality of writing a book in two languages as has so often been done by Scots writers hitherto. Scots speakers are accustomed to hearing that their language is declining and teachers and academics may hark back to the Golden Age of Scots in the fifteenth and sixteenth centuries. Fitt is projecting Scots into the future as a vivid and robust language. In so doing he presents us with another challenge. He makes us re-examine the language we use today. Instead of seeing it as comfortable, couthy and backward looking, we see its potential. By looking at old words in new contexts, we look freshly and more deeply at meanings. The close engagement that the novel stimulates between the reader and the Scots language is one of the many things that makes the novel much more than just a good yarn and distinguishes Fitt as a craftsman with words or, to use the Scots term, a makar.

FURTHER READING

Antczak, J., *Science Fiction: The Mythos of a New Romance*, Neal-Schuman, London, 1985.

Jago, M., *Living Language: Language and Style*, Hodder & Stoughton, London, 1999.

McMahon, A., *An Introduction to English Phonology*, Edinburgh University Press, Edinburgh, 2002.

Robertson, J., *The Smoky Smirr o Rain*, Itchy Coo, Edinburgh, 2003.

Robinson, C. & C-A Crawford, *Scotspeak*, Scots Language Resource Centre, Perth, 2000.

Robinson, M., *Concise Scots Dictionary*, Edinburgh University Press, Edinburgh, 1985.

Texts for comparison

Banks, I., *The Bridge*, Abacus, London, 1992.

Gibson, W., *Neuromancer*, Voyager, London 1995.

Grassic Gibbon, L., *A Scots Quair*, Canongate, Edinburgh, 1995.

Henryson, R., *The Testament of Cresseid* (ed. H. MacDiarmid), Penguin, Harmondsworth, 1988.

Rankin, I., *Rebus: The Early Years*, Orion, 2000.

Orwell. G., *Nineteen Eighty-four*, Penguin, Harmondsworth, 2002.

Welsh, I., *Trainspotting*, Vintage, 2004.